"Todd Mealy's *This Is the Rat Spea* [barcode] historiography of the modern Africa MW00929359 examines the nascent organization and complicated dynamics of protest and resistance at Franklin and Marshall College in Lancaster, Pennsylvania, during the 1960s, brilliantly burrowing beneath the sweeping national narratives of civil rights and peace protest to reveal the who, what, when, and how ordinary individuals, operating in extraordinary times, actually built the movement on the ground. Mealy deftly reveals that on the micro level, the goals of the national movement were not universal, and that local strategies often underwent frequent political and social change as students, professors, college administrators, and communities struggled together—and often at cross purposes—to answer the call for equality and freedom. A must-read!"

—*Kate Clifford Larson, Ph.D., author of Rosemary, The Hidden Kennedy Daughter; Bound For the Promised Land: Harriet Tubman, Portrait of an American Hero; and The Assassin's Accomplice: Mary Surratt and the Plot to Kill Abraham Lincoln*

"Todd Mealy's work presents a painstaking and well-researched recounting of the events of May 22, 1969, and the circumstances preceding them. In an era following the 1965 "Moynihan Report," the events at F&M represented the importance of not only talking about the African American experience but listening to the unique voice of black Americans. The African American community wanted more than just to be talked about—it demanded to be talked to. While the perspectives of those involved may differ in emphasis and role, one thing still remains clear after forty-seven years—if black lives matter today, then their unique voice must still be heard."

—*LeRoy Pernell, '71, professor of law and former dean, Florida Agricultural and Mechanical University College of Law, former dean and professor emeritus, Northern Illinois University College of Law, former vice provost for minority affairs, the Ohio State University*

"Todd Mealy's deeply sourced study of black power at a small liberal arts college adds measurably to the new scholarship on black student activism in the long sixties."

—*Van Gosse, associate professor of history at Franklin and Marshall College*

Also by TODD M. MEALY

Biography of an Antislavery City: Antislavery Activists, Abolitionists, and Underground Railroad Operatives in Harrisburg, PA

Aliened American: A Biography of William Howard Day, 1825–1900 (published in two volumes)

Legendary Locals of Harrisburg

This Is the Rat Speaking

Black Power and the Promise of Racial
Consciousness at Franklin and Marshall
College in the Age of the Takeover,

1967–69

Todd M. Mealy

Foreword by Dr. Benjamin P. Bowser

THIS IS THE RAT SPEAKING
BLACK POWER AND THE PROMISE OF RACIAL
CONSCIOUSNESS AT FRANKLIN AND MARSHALL
COLLEGE IN THE AGE OF THE TAKEOVER, 1967–69

iUniverse books may be ordered through booksellers or by contacting:

iUniverse
1663 Liberty Drive
Bloomington, IN 47403
www.iuniverse.com
1-800-Authors (1-800-288-4677)

Because of the dynamic nature of the Internet, any web addresses or links contained in this book may have changed since publication and may no longer be valid. The views expressed in this work are solely those of the author and do not necessarily reflect the views of the publisher, and the publisher hereby disclaims any responsibility for them.

Any people depicted in stock imagery provided by Thinkstock are models, and such images are being used for illustrative purposes only. Certain stock imagery © Thinkstock.

ISBN: 978-1-5320-1033-0 (sc)
ISBN: 978-1-5320-1034-7 (e)

Library of Congress Control Number: 2016921364

Print information available on the last page.

iUniverse rev. date: 03/23/2017

To my son, Carter

Most people grapple with issues concerning race in the United States of America. Make an effort to understand these matters, for race is at the heart of US history and culture.

CONTENTS

ILLUSTRATIONS

FOREWORD

D O NOT BE misled. *This Is the Rat Speaking* is not just about Lancaster, Pennsylvania, Franklin and Marshall College, or events at either place forty-five years ago. Todd M. Mealy does a masterful job of using the city and college as case studies of why young men and women riot and protest. He digs down through layers of memories, defenses, anger, and still raw trauma to provide the reader with safe passage through a period and events that are as timely now as they were then. What unfolded in Lancaster in 1967–69 might as well be what is happening today in Ferguson, Baltimore, or Chicago—or, for that matter, Paris in 1789 or Boston in 1773.

Lancaster in the late 1960s seemed a long way physically and spiritually from Harlem or Detroit. It was a small city, and a classical community in the sense that people had intimate day-to-day contact with one another. It was a model of Émile Durkheim's organic solidarity and the opposite of large and densely populated and impersonal cities. This is not where you would imagine riot and protest. When I first walked into Lancaster's Seventh Ward in 1965, I stood in its very heart looking for a ghetto. There were only two signs that this was the place: it was run-down in relation to the rest of Lancaster, and black people lived there. Wherever ghettoes are, they are first psychological, in the minds of residents and nonresidents alike, and are imposed on those who live within them. Their physical condition is only a reflection of these facts. Everyone in Lancaster except me knew the Seventh Ward's boundaries, what they meant, and who was supposed to be in and outside them, just as I know where the ghettoes' lines are and their meaning in New York.

But what was not appreciated about Lancaster is that it sits on a historical fault line. Forty-five years ago was not the first time there was an eruption of disorder in Lancaster County. By 1850, one of the largest concentrations of free African Americans lived in the county. It was a haven for runaway slaves, fewer than one hundred miles from Maryland and the Mason–Dixon line separating free from slave. Soon after the passage of the Second Fugitive Slave Act in 1850, Edward Gorsuch led a group of riders over that line to Christiana in Lancaster County to reenslave his runaways. He was killed in the ensuing struggle. The black defenders were tried and were found *not* guilty of killing a white man, to the shock of the entire nation. This was called the Christiana Riot and was one of the events that led to the American Civil War.

The ghosts of the Christiana Riot came back in 1967–69. Blacks "rioted" then as they are doing now. But in 1968, it was not about their basic freedom; it was about the value of that freedom. Taken-for-granted racial segregation, job discrimination, and police brutality, and the presumption of inferiority, negate the personal freedom former slaves fought for over a century ago. Even in Lancaster, as in the rest of the nation, ordinary young men and women who came of age found their humanity so denied that they could bespeak of themselves as "rats"—trapped in a ghetto. But the irony of Mealy's reconstruct is that the white mayor, police, school officials, and students were trapped as well. They too found their world turned upside down and found themselves baffled over what had happened and why, as is the case today.

Through in-depth interviews and a thorough review of documents, Mealy is able to reconstruct the times, the people, and their circumstances with frightening clarity. We relive their experiences, but this time we learn what they thought, what they reflected upon, and the secrets they could not tell then. When reflective studies are done of the current riots, those researchers will find what Mealy has already told us from the last time.

There is more. Ghettoes are gritty places that are short on hope and on a sense of future. College and university communities are the opposite. But in this provocative story, Mealy explores not just any college or university. At Franklin and Marshall College (F&M), students are not identification numbers, teaching units, or faces in large classrooms. Faculty know their name, ask them questions and expect studied answers, and work with them one-on-one in and outside of classes. The dean and president know their names, as well as where they are from and what each of their personal challenges are. The college was a rich, intensive liberal arts setting then as it is now.

Yet in the 1960s, there were two, contradictory F&Ms. There was the academic F&M that was about faculty contact. The other F&M consisted of fraternities that were the extracurricular life of the college. Most fraternity brothers were crude racists, were sexually abusive of women, and were contradictions who should have been embarrassments to the academic F&M. Black students were admitted to the first F&M, but not to the second. (No one in their right mind would want to be part of that savagery even if they could.) Despite the college's high-minded mission, black students at F&M were as segregated and ghettoized outside of classes as their peers were in Lancaster City.

Several faculty, as if riding across the Mason–Dixon line, called the Christiana ghosts to campus. They unwittingly rendered invisible and inferior the black students whom they knew personally and as students, by using them as class exhibits for their white peers in the college's first black studies course. Mealy aptly captures what this intimate betrayal felt like. In the only F&M that black students were part of, the academic, they were reduced like their community peers to "rats speaking." So even under the best circumstances, the ghosts of Christiana had to also visit F&M.

Lancaster is now a racially diverse metropolitan area in its own right. The academic F&M has broken the stranglehold of all-male white fraternities over the extracurricular life of the college. The college is academically better for it, socially richer, and wonderfully coed. Perhaps the Christiana ghosts no longer need to return to either F&M. *This Is the Rat Speaking* turns out to be an overdue vindication for a group of young men (and women) who embodied the ghosts of Christiana in both Lancaster and F&M forty-five years ago. Virtually every one of the black student demands that the college put off back in 1969 are now intrinsic parts of the college's profile of itself as a high-quality social and academic institution. It turns out that the rats spoke and were visionaries.

This Is the Rat Speaking is a real page-turner. Get ready for an adventure and a window into the past and present.

Dr. Benjamin P. Bowser

September 2016

ACKNOWLEDGMENTS

IN MANY WAYS, *This Is the Rat Speaking* is the product of the personal relationships I developed while living in Lancaster, Pennsylvania. In 2001, I moved to Lancaster by way of Harrisburg and began teaching at the city's high school. My boss that first year was Leon "Buddy" Glover, an educator whom I consider to be one of Lancaster's finest heroes. Glover deserves special credit for his willingness to guide me as a public school teacher and civil rights enthusiast. This one's for you, Buddy.

Along the way, I benefited greatly from interviewing many remarkable individuals, namely, Lewis H. Myers, Benjamin P. Bowser, LeRoy Pernell, James Craighead, Harold Dunbar, Elizabeth Ford, retired Lancaster City Police Officer J. Donald Schaeffer, retired Lancaster County Commissioner Ron Ford, Louis Butcher, Gerald Wilson, Leroy Hopkins, Stanley Michalak, and Pauline Pittenger. Of that group, I am especially indebted to Dr. Bowser, who advised me throughout the project. Retired Franklin and Marshall professors Donald J. Tyrrell and Leon Galis provided much needed insight along the way. The late Benjamin Bethea was graciously willing to share his contentious story as an agent of Lancaster's activist Black Arise group.

I would make a colossal mistake if I failed to acknowledge Nelson Polite Jr., Shirley Lucas Gillis, and Hazel Jackson, three civil rights pioneers who passed away during the writing of this book, as well as Sumner Bohee, the first African American to graduate from Franklin and Marshall College. Corey Conyers, Catherine Sturla, Mushtak Meherzad, and Mariah Mamas provided assistance in the very early stages of this project. Alas, I want to give thanks to my two advisers at the Pennsylvania State University–Harrisburg, Dr. Michael Barton and Dr. Charles Kupfer, for supporting the research of this profound topic.

Writing nonfiction is always a challenge, especially when it demands the laborious process of conducting interviews. Therefore, a very special thank-you is due to my wife, Melissa, for her encouragement and for allowing me to take the time necessary to complete this project. We have both made many new friends along the way.

INTRODUCTION

M AY 22, 1969. It was a Thursday morning on the campus of
Franklin and Marshall College, a small but prestigious liberal
arts school located in rural Lancaster County, Pennsylvania. Before
eight o'clock in the morning, more than sixty people, most of whom
were African American students at the school, had gathered in front
of Old Main, the college's oldest building, and Goethean Hall to
boycott the final exam of a course called Interdepartmental-4: The
Black Experience in America. The campus had witnessed few events
quite like the situation that was unfolding on the courtyard in the
center of campus. During five hours of rich confusion, as well as wild
contradictions, the small boycott escalated into a hostage taking. For
several hours, African American protestors, some brandishing chair
legs and walkie-talkies, detained seven professors against their will
inside Goethean Hall.

The disturbance began as students of the Afro-American Society
cordoned off the entrance to Old Main, where the examination was
to be administered. When the professors of the course turned the
exam into a take-home test, the students confronted their white

counterparts by destroying the test booklets. The situation grew more contentious when, as the professors walked to the adjacent Goethean Hall to escape the disturbance, several of the boycotters blocked the doors leading in and out of the building. The professors were incarcerated inside Goethean's seminar room. The students barricaded the front door with a small mound of desks and chairs. Men holding walkie-talkies guarded the back door. Demonstrators outside secured the windows.

While inside Goethean Hall, the students presented their demands. First, they insisted on the creation of an interdisciplinary black studies department that would award an academic minor while offering a comprehensive curriculum integrating cultural studies across academic fields, combining history, art, psychology, and literature with practical field experiences that placed students in America's black communities. Second, the students demanded that the college hire black faculty members. Third, the students insisted that an all-black fraternity house be inserted into the Greek system. As for the black students enrolled in the Interdepartmental-4: The Black Experience in America course, since the professors used them as classroom props during the semester, they accordingly demanded an apology. As the testimonial from the boycotters suggests, the students felt they were treated like laboratory rats for their white counterparts to study. Another demand insisted on exemption from the final exam. They each wanted an A since they had, in fact, lived the black experience in America and were forced to share those experiences with their white peers. "For all of our efforts, time and goodwill we received not even a little bit of gratification," proclaimed the students. "This is the rat speaking and all you motherfuckers can go to hell!"[1]

Large or small, the uprising at Franklin and Marshall was not the nation's first. Boycotts and sit-ins, even takeovers of administrative buildings on the United States' campuses, were taking place across the country months before Franklin and Marshall's disturbance that spring morning. Colleges and universities like San Francisco State, Brandeis, Swarthmore, Duke, Rutgers–Newark, Stanford, Wisconsin–Madison, Louisville, City College of New York, Howard, Columbia, and Cornell endured respective episodes of building seizures by impassioned African American students, a growing demographic of baby boomers representing the New Black Left. Of those aforementioned, Cornell's incident was the most brazen. There in Ithaca, on April 19, 1969, more than one hundred African American students took over Willard Straight Hall. Fifteen hours into the takeover, once groups of white students threatened to attack the black students occupying the dormitory, rifles, shotguns, and hatchets were delivered to the demonstrators. Soon images of black students brandishing semiautomatic rifles and bullet belts were captured on television screens across the country. After thirty-six hours, the standoff ended when university administrators gave in to the demands of the students, who, like those at Franklin and Marshall, were demanding the creation of a black studies department and better housing for minority students off campus.

With plotlines rivaling others across the country, Franklin and Marshall's May 22 uprising appears to be unique in important respects. It is the only episode that witnessed several of the college's professors taken as hostages. It is the only episode where a college administration later rescinded its deal made with the students. Similar to other episodes, the students who were involved in the disturbance at Franklin and Marshall avoided legal ramifications.

The new action of taking over an administrative building was part of a broader transformation in the cultural response to many urban riots, including the 1965 upheaval in Watts, the Vietnam War, the assassination of Malcolm X, and the near assassination of James Meredith, that penetrated African American society. The seventy African American students who took control of Ford and Sydeman Halls at Brandeis University on January 8, 1969, explained their behavior as representative of an attack against a certain power structure—in this case, the college or university. Thus, taking over a building empowered a previously powerless entity on campus. Journalist and African American studies professor Marc Lamont Hill suggests this would be the moment when "nobody" became "somebody." "At every moment in history, oppression has been met with resistance," Hill writes in his 2016 tome *Nobody: Casualties of America's War on the Vulnerable, from Ferguson to Flint and Beyond*, adding that in every case when an established power has relegated vulnerable people to a second-class or alienated status, "the People have asserted that they are, in fact, Somebody."[2] Therefore, the action of taking over a building removed power from the hands of the college faculty and gave it to the students until change was effected. In the case of an overwhelmingly white campus like the one at Franklin and Marshall College in 1969, the omission of curriculum centered on African and African American culture, the absence of a black fraternity, the exclusion of African Americans from student activities and social gatherings, and the lack of black faculty deprived its students of color of the cultural development that has always been considered an integral part of the liberal arts experience. Moreover, building seizures were a new form of protest. The act alone was frightening. It consequently garnered greater attention to the cause. Therefore, this decades-old conflict that took place in rural Lancaster County, small by most measures of historical importance, possesses great relevance for many racial issues afflicting the United States in the twenty-first century, including the arguments set forth by activists in the Black Lives Matter movement.

Sociologist Eddie S. Glaude Jr. suggests that the crisis engulfing the United States has always been the way society values black lives, especially at critical moments in our nation's history. Glaude writes in *Democracy in Black* that during those times when "fundamental changes" regarding race have occurred in the United States, "white people are valued more than others." He calls the black–white appreciation disparity the "value gap," which "limits the scope of change" toward a postracial and postracist society. This gap was first widened after the Civil War when reconstruction efforts that endeavored to create a postracist society were sullied by the enactment of Jim Crow laws that beat people of color back into submission for the century that followed. Glaude's theory also applies to the history of welfare in this country. He notes that from Franklin Roosevelt's New Deal to the year when New Black Leftists began occupying college buildings—a time recognized for the increase of black welfare recipients—"welfare was widely seen as good government ... But around 1968," he laments, "the face of poverty turned black, and [suddenly] welfare became a problem of government dependence."[3] In education, the value gap persisted at every level during the first three-quarters of the twentieth-century, in part because of administrative refusal to see things from the perspective of African American students who were choosing to enroll in predominantly white liberal arts schools instead of historically black colleges and universities. Liberal arts colleges drew students of color because those institutions were seen as bastions of democratic life, but other than making a palpable effort to recruit black students to their respective institutions of higher learning, very few actually made fundamental changes to close the gap of inequality on campus.[4]

The uprising at Franklin and Marshall would not have taken place if a swarm of activists had not paved the way, and if audacious students with imperfect methods of commandeering intercollegiate curriculum had not taken risks. Black Leftist leaders like Stokely Carmichael and Malcolm X, and before them, figures like W. E. B. Du Bois, Marcus Garvey, and Frederick Douglass, did not strike out to create a postracial society. Award-winning author Michael Eric Dyson keenly points out, "A post-racial outlook seeks to ignore, or destroy, race." He writes, "Post-race is really black disappearance."[5] Rather, the black power movement's goal, since it emerged on the heels of the civil rights movement, was to unmask white privilege in controversial ways like reveling in black pride, occupying college administration buildings, or wearing berets and black leather jackets while guarding the neighborhood from state violence: all to say, according to Dyson, that "black folks should not have to stop being black to be seen as fully human" or, for that matter, to advocate for a college degree program that focused on black culture.

This Is the Rat Speaking addresses five principal questions: What factors explain the dramatic changes in racial attitudes and behavior that occurred in Lancaster, Pennsylvania, between 1967 and 1969? What factors explain the radicalization of local African American civil rights activists? How much did such radicalization in Lancaster reflect the larger world of race relations? How did all of this gain a foothold on Franklin and Marshall's campus? And, what steps should Franklin and Marshall have taken to close the value gap between its white and black students?

To qualify, *This Is the Rat Speaking* makes no judgments about the people involved in the cases mentioned herein. It seeks to describe the events as they happened and to interpret how the activists of the era were motivated to take such audacious measures. And it is clear that African Americans at Franklin and Marshall College possessed mixed emotions over the level of extremism coming from activists living in the nearby city. There is a transparent distinction between black power activists who mobilized themselves against the racist power structure in Lancaster and those who used nonviolent methods. Particularly nonviolent is the foundational topic of *This Is the Rat Speaking*, namely, the May 22 uprising at Franklin and Marshall College, where, unlike the episode at Cornell University, except for broken legs off of chairs, not a weapon was found at the scene.

No disparaging effort is intended toward the college or the people involved when the May 22 uprising is discussed in this book. The terms *incarceration, hostage, sit-in, strike, boycott, disturbance,* and *uprising* are each used to describe the episode, not as an effort to insult or seem insolent. After interviewing many of people who were there, in addition to having discussions with archivists at the college, and after I read countless transcripts about the crisis, I found that there is no consensus on what to call the event. The present leadership at Franklin and Marshall call it a strike. Those who were directly involved have called it both a boycott and a sit-in. The professors who were interviewed, and students who attended the college but were not part of the demonstration, have called it an incarceration and a hostage crisis. I have simply tried to sort through the various factors and have decided to call it an uprising. The May 22 uprising included both a boycott (students refused to take the final exam) and a hostage taking (professors were detained against their free will).

In analyzing Franklin and Marshall's first major racial confrontation, I had to consider several peripheral issues while writing *This Is the Rat Speaking*. Those who read these words should at least realize these considerations. It has been almost fifty years since the episodes discussed herein took place. Interviews are the most valuable source of evidence, yet many details have been forgotten. In other cases, some people wished to overlook certain pieces of information for fear of self-incrimination. I have promised each of my interview subjects that I will be mindful and professional about any and all information that they disclosed over the course of the interviews, and how I divulge it in this text. Yet actions have consequences. Many of the people I interviewed are upstanding citizens who have gone on to become important leaders in their respective professions after having been involved, in one way or another, in radical events almost five decades ago. So I understand their apprehension about divulging certain details with someone they hardly know.

During the weeks after the uprising, the college's president formed a team to identify how Franklin and Marshall found itself in such a predicament and to offer solutions to remove all forms of institutional racism. A committee of professors, college students, and Lancaster City community leaders was charged with taking testimonies from witnesses, examining the demographics of the college and its connection to Lancaster City, interpreting the social relationships between white and black students on campus—especially concerning the size and influence of Franklin and Marshall's (de facto) segregated Greek fraternities—and evaluating the interaction between professors and students. Though the investigative committee should be applauded for its work in revealing a multitude of institutional problems that endured on campus, the endeavor did not result in reconciliation. The maladroit episode blackened Franklin and Marshall's reputation for many months. It left several of the professors, whose lives had been dedicated to social justice, dismayed and heartbroken. Conversely, many of the black students, graduates and underclassmen alike, thereafter felt alienated by their peers and utterly abandoned by the college.

The silver lining of the May 22 uprising was that it brought awareness of the racial anguish that also existed across the rest of the country. It offers profound insight into how far committed activists, young as well as educated, were willing to go to create an identity of their own in an environment that made them feel out of place. In charting the sweeping events that brought Franklin and Marshall College's African American students into upheaval, it is customary to focus on milestones of social change or calamities of social justice such as the violence at the Edmund Pettus Bridge, the assassination of Martin Luther King Jr., and black student protests at San Francisco State, Columbia, Cornell, and other universities. Measured up against these landmark events, the drama at Franklin and Marshall is easily overlooked, pushed aside by more pressing episodes yet to come. Nevertheless, *This Is the Rat Speaking* will bring to light the thoughts, motivations, and actions that explain the black experience in a small but essential region of the United States, and the social and educational changes that came with it.

Chapter 1
THE TOWN

L ONG BEFORE THE scene in front of Old Main and Goethean Hall dirtied the image of Franklin and Marshall College, there was a demand to diversify the student body. As the sixties dawned, the private Lancaster County college boasted a heterogeneous enrollment that was rivaled by few liberal arts colleges in Pennsylvania. Franklin and Marshall enjoyed a noble reputation as one of the earliest small liberal arts colleges to aggressively recruit students of color. Most of its black students arrived from urban centers in the Mid-Atlantic, while a fair percentage arrived from southern cities like Washington, DC, and St. Petersburg, Florida.*

Owing to this fact, most faculty and students contended that their college exceeded the level of racial understanding held by most colleges and universities of the era. But it is important to understand

---

* A number of articles published in recent years brood over the District of Columbia's "Southernness." While the city might be considered part of the North by twenty-first-century standards because of political, cultural, and historical reasons, the nation's capital is included in this book as a Southern locale. Historically, the city had few so-called Jim Crow laws in the lead up to the sixties. However, the few laws that did exist allowed segregated public schools and recreation facilities.

the historical irony that diversification produced. As Franklin and Marshall opened its classrooms and dormitories to nonwhite students, the dialogue about issues regarding racial injustice among students on campus ought to have increased. With diversification came the demand for new interdisciplinary academic models centered on cultural divisions. By 1967, virtually all of Franklin and Marshall's black students were advocating for programs that concentrated on cultural awareness, especially those who felt out of place by the overwhelming white student body and the unfamiliar agricultural lifestyle that living in Lancaster County presented. The requests by the students were quite extensive. An off-campus house topped the list. On a campus where there were nearly a dozen all-white fraternities, such a house could serve as the fraternal residence for the school's black students. In theory, this could have allowed for an extension of the black communities from where the students had come. Other demands called for a black studies department that provided courses in history, literature, art, economics, race theory, anthropology, and sociological fieldwork. With that, the hiring of more minority professors and advisers was requested.

As the frenzy around black empowerment mounted at Franklin and Marshall College during the second half of the sixties, the impatience of the college's African Americans in their challenge of the administration to make changes intensified. The black student community found inspiration in a new, more radical tone. In June 1966, fewer than two weeks after James Meredith was shot while embarking on a two-hundred-mile walk from Memphis, Tennessee, to Jackson, Mississippi, in a demonstration of courage over the cult of fear that had so long polluted the Jim Crow South, Stokely Carmichael, the current president of the Student Nonviolent Coordinating Committee, demanded "black power." "The only way we're going to stop them white men from whipping us is to take over. We've been saying freedom for six years," he said. "What we're going to start saying now is 'black power!' What do you want?" he asked a crowd that had gathered at Broad Street Park in Greenwood, Mississippi, to hear him speak.

"Black power!" the audience echoed.

A Howard University graduate, Carmichael explicated his call for black power in an article entitled "What We Want." He wrote the following:

> Black power will mean that if a Negro is elected sheriff, he can end police brutality. If a black man is elected tax assessor, he can collect and channel funds for the building of better roads and schools serving black people—thus advancing the move from political power into the economic arena ... It means the creation of power bases from which black people can work to change statewide or nationwide patterns of oppression through pressure from strength—instead of weakness.

Carmichael called for the resegregation of American society, claiming that no political party or predominantly white police department worked for the enfranchisement and protection of black Americans. He lamented further, "It was the call for them to define their own goals, lead their own organizations, and create their own power bases from which they could change the patterns of oppression."[1] Though his position on black power confused most leading civil rights figures—when asked by the media what Carmichael meant by black power, Martin Luther King said, "I think it's an unfortunate choice of words," while Ray Wilkins of the National Association for the Advancement of Colored People explained his contempt for black power by denouncing it as "a reverse Hitler, a reverse Ku

Klux Klan"—Carmichael offered very concrete things: an end to inferior education; an end to systemic racism, otherwise referred to as de facto segregation; an end to economic domination; an end to exclusion from the political process; and an end to racist terrorism often perpetrated by the police and members of the Ku Klux Klan.[2]

Carmichael's black liberation ideology took hold a few months later. Though it was not his Student Nonviolent Coordinating Committee that led the struggle, in October 1966, Bobby Seale and Huey Newton, two students at Oakland's Merritt College, formed the Black Panther Party. Encompassing a ten-point plan advising black leaders throughout the country on how to lead their respective black neighborhoods, the Black Panthers reinforced Carmichael's call for black solidarity by insisting on economic and military control of the United States' black neighborhoods. "If we have no control of the destiny of the institutions within our community, then we have no guarantee of any other political rights," proclaimed Newton.[3] Their philosophy was buttressed by a socialist ideology that enabled them to defend their community from white aggressors while simultaneously acknowledging themselves as a colony of capitalistic America. That attitude found a ready audience from African American students who were caught up in the revolutionary mood induced by the violence befallen on the black community after the passage of the major civil rights legislations desegregated the country. Certainly, African Americans at Franklin and Marshall favored Carmichael and Newton's doctrine of self-determination, thereafter insisting that the college's curricula had to focus on issues relevant to real circumstances that emerged in the daily lives of blacks living in the United States. This kind of dialogue was long overdue at Franklin and Marshall.

Carmichael and Newton's revolutionary philosophy offered an

attractive alternative for young African Americans as they left their homes and went off to Lancaster County, Pennsylvania. To find comfort while away from home for the first time, it only made sense that black men on campus found solace in the New Black Left doctrine permeating from activists in the city. Some students became involved in citywide elections by campaigning for black power or antiwar candidates who were sympathetic to their views. A small number of activists were elected to the college's student government and obtained positions writing for the college's newspaper. Others campaigned for lowering the voting age to eighteen. Many volunteered for antipoverty programs that reached out to children from dysfunctional families and disadvantaged academic environments. Everyone involved wanted to reach out to the black residents living in Lancaster City's poorest and most segregated region: the Seventh Ward.

The city around Franklin and Marshall College was a noisy and crowded jumble of activism inspired by the clashing doctrines of Martin Luther King's tactical nonviolence and Carmichael's black power. Lancaster, located in south central Pennsylvania, is popularly known as the bedrock of Pennsylvania Dutch Country. Manufacturing was its chief industry. The Amish were (and still are considered) its signature attraction. Yet by 1967, the rural character of the area had been utterly overshadowed by a city with social lines racially divided. There were over fifty thousand people living in the city; about three thousand, or 5 percent, were African American.[4]

The city of Lancaster was intersected by Queen and King Streets, which debouched into four squared zones. The street dividing the city vertically at its center was Queen. King Street ran horizontally. Each zone shared unique characteristics that distinguished one from the other. The southwestern part of Lancaster was called Cabbage Hill. It was the heart of Lancaster's German American population, bustling with bootleggers and speakeasies during Prohibition. The northwest was the city's affluent section, housing two signature businesses: Armstrong World Industries and R. R. Donnelly Printing. Franklin and Marshall College also lay within the city's northwest. The college employed people from various backgrounds, so the campus was one of the most liberal areas in town. "The ethnic mix leads to some odd combinations, like Spanish-speaking Mennonites," said one college student.[5] Lancaster's northeast is the most historic district. The area claims the oldest farmers' market in the United States. The northeast, in addition, contained most of the city's law offices, entrepreneurs, and saloons. Lancastrians flocked to the northeast district for its four movie theaters and public parks. The YMCA was a familiar landmark in the area, as was the city's train station. It was along King Street where fights were almost constant occurrences, especially during the world wars when loyalties between German and non-German residents clashed.

Few parts of the city appeared as uninviting as the southeast. This area included the Seventh Ward. It was a beyond-belief blighted and racially segregated area often branded the Bucket of Blood or Bloody Seventh. "Life is less formal here," one resident said. "You can hold shouting matches at 3:00 a.m. or wrestle in the street whenever you want. Only sissies pull the car over in the Ward, so double-parking is de rigueur. Slumlords are absent, and often jack up rent for no apparent reason."[6] Since World War II, African Americans owned restaurants, medical practices, barbershops, and other small businesses in the area. An unparalleled sense of pride existed there as neighbors shared duties of punishing the community's youngsters. The Bethel African Methodist Episcopal and Ebenezer Baptist Churches served the spiritual and civic needs of residents. It was a sovereign yet deprived neighborhood in the fifties and sixties.

The Seventh Ward was comprised, roughly, of the territory bounded by Church Street on the west, Lime Street to the north, Dauphin Street to the east, and Strawberry Street on the south. Its major artery was South Duke Street, which ran north and south. At its western edge was the ward's purlieus Five Points, where South Duke, Church, and Farnum Streets intersected. In the years immediately following World War II, Jews and African Americans shared the area. Just off South Duke and Chester Streets was the Congregation Degal Israel synagogue. Owing to Jewish doctrine, the area around the Orthodox synagogue housed hundreds of Jewish residents. There were several tree lines throughout the ward, especially along Christian, Dauphin, Woodward, and Green Streets.

The most recognizable road in the Seventh Ward was Green Street, a very short thoroughfare that ran north from Strawberry Street across the base of the southeast to South Duke Street. Most of the area's African American leaders lived on or around Green Street, including US Olympic champion Henry Norwood "Barney" Ewell. Most of the houses on Green Street were brick or stone with concrete stoops, each topped with a gable roof and fronted by a walkway. As sacred as Green Street still is to Lancastrians, it was overbuilt and provided limited accessible space for recreation. Near Green Street were Barney Google Row's substandard housing development and automotive dump between Juniata and Susquehanna Streets and along the 700 block of Southeast Avenue. The brand new Higbee Elementary School on North, Rockland, and Dauphin Streets sat adjacent to Green Street.

On the southern edge of the Seventh Ward, where North and Strawberry Streets intersected, stood the historic Bethel AME Church. Aside from the Crispus Attucks Community Center, located on Howard Avenue, the church was the nexus of Seventh Ward social life. The city chapter of the NAACP used the Bethel AME Church as its headquarters.

David Schuyler reports in *A City Transformed: Redevelopment, Race, and Suburbanization in Lancaster, Pennsylvania, 1940–1980* (2002) that 96 percent of Lancaster's African American population lived in the Seventh Ward. Schuyler reports that to a degree, local redlining practices were responsible for the city's racial and socioeconomic divisions.[7] By the sixties, the loss of jobs and businesses in the Seventh Ward's lower-income and minority-based neighborhood was a stain on the city. Not even genuine attempts at redevelopment could wipe that away. Banks and credit firms simply refused to invest in the area. The disregard by lenders—whether of minority-owned businesses or white-owned firms located in the ward—accentuated racial solidarity in the community, thus impeding even further the possibility of interracial harmony.

From the outside, it looked as if African American residents blighted the area of the city they inhabited. This was not true, of course. The neighborhood was generally run-down before their arrival. Lancaster's southeast had historically been a dumping ground wrought with trash heaps, ash dumps, and automotive stations, which presented serious environmental nuisances. As early as 1944, the Lancaster Housing Committee of the Post-War Planning Council declared 85 percent of the dwellings occupied by the Seventh Ward's African Americans as substandard or "decayed," claiming further that the units in the ward were unsafe, unsanitary, and a hazard to the safety, health, and welfare of the inhabitants. The area was densely populated with no open space for common playgrounds, and no place to park cars along the street. Landlords bestowed few improvements, actually allowing the area to deteriorate further. In addition, excessive rents and exclusion from adjoining vicinities overcrowded Seventh Warders both in their homes and on their blocks.

Since hundreds of poor residents constituted the majority of Lancaster's black citizenry, the Bloody Seventh became the local nucleus for the black power cause. "There were hard lines that the blacks didn't pass over [into] the white part of town," recalls Benjamin Bethea, a black power activist from Lancaster City, "and the whites didn't go to the black part of town."[8] Within the Seventh Ward's abstract borders, neighbors connected with one another, but outsiders were at risk. People of color generally chose not to leave the southeast area after dark. Likewise, the people from bordering neighborhoods chose not to enter the Seventh Ward after sunset. "If we ventured past any of those streets, north to west, east and south, we would have trouble," Bethea acknowledged. Locals considered the ward the city's Harlem, Bedford-Stuyvesant, or Watts.

Lancaster was a long way from New York and Los Angeles, but it was an area that fully met criteria for urban redevelopment. David Schuyler claims that in 1959, 32 percent of the Seventh Ward's structures, or 780 buildings, were "dilapidated and substandard," while 10 percent, or 278 buildings, "lacked running water."[9] Starting in 1959, the Lancaster Redevelopment Authority—assigned with the hefty task of eradicating the slums—started construction on twelve blocks containing 397 residential, industrial, community, and commercial structures in the southeast. The area under redevelopment, Schuyler describes, included "Church Street south along the east side of Duke Street to Juniata and ... most of the blocks on the west side between North and Juniata Streets." On three of these blocks, Schuyler reports, "70-percent of the structures were occupied by non-white residents; five other blocks had a nonwhite population of 30-percent or more."[10] Between 1959 and 1969, the area looked like a combat zone, as beautiful brick homes were knocked down and fields were tattered for the construction of projects like the South Duke Street expressway, the new Higbee Elementary School, the Susquehanna Court Apartments, Bogar Houses, the Lancaster Boys Club, and the Faith United Church of Christ.[11] It was a rotting society that was becoming increasingly ready for a makeover.

The Redevelopment Authority tried in earnest to desegregate the Seventh Ward. The authority hired several Philadelphia housing consultants to transform the southeast into a harmonious community. Consultant Drayton S. Bryant prepared the plan for the area's redevelopment. In a statement, Bryant said, "Renewal should not create a new and heavier 'lock-in' of low-income families in the same area," but instead should attract a "wide range of people." Bryant wanted to build housing "appropriate to different economic levels and for individuals and families at different states of life."[12] To accomplish his vision of mixing high-income residents with traditional Seventh Warders, Bryant needed to demolish many of the area's original buildings only to construct a new commercial square, several housing complexes, and a community center. The area already had a plaza on Duke Street that it could build upon. The Duke Plaza, since 1963, operated as a retail center for area residents. Bryant suggested that it could attract non–Seventh Warders if it were to be expanded into a thirty-five-thousand-square-foot shopping mall by acquiring the tract of land along South Duke Street between Chester and North Streets. In all, he proposed a 1.6-acre site that would include parking lots and a comfortably shaded recreational park that, as he implied, would function as "a combination of the commercial and the public that had long characterized cities but that was being lost in private suburban shopping malls."[13] Bryant wanted to build apartment buildings near the commercial square and call them the South Park Towers. The towers were supposed to include up to four apartment buildings on a tract of land between Chesapeake and South Duke Streets. Finally, Bryant hoped to erect a new multipurpose community center on South Duke Street. By placing the community center on Duke Street, he hoped it might attract permanent newcomers.

Ground was broken for Bryant's projects in 1967. But after ten years, twice the time he projected as necessary to complete his plans, not one unit of the family housing units that he'd designed had been built in the project area. Bryant's community center was never completed. The extension of the South Duke Street expressway and the Duke Street Mall were his greatest accomplishments, but even those resulted in only slight improvements.[14] "Very stable families, particularly on South Duke Street, lost their homes [for construction projects]," recalls Seventh Ward resident Ronald Ford, who later became Lancaster's first African American city council president and Lancaster county commissioner. Ford noted the loss of many affluent whites and African Americans because of redevelopment assignments. "The more mobile African American families moved out of that part of the city," he said, adding, "Whites fled as a result of urban renewal too."[15] After all the efforts made by the Redevelopment Authority, many pockets within the Seventh Ward looked as underdeveloped and segregated as they had before the construction. However buried or repressed, vengeful emotions in town were activated by this negligence.

Chapter 2

THE STRUGGLE

The limitations of southeast Lancaster were by no means restricted to Seventh Ward borders. Socially accepted forms of segregation were a very real and ubiquitous part of Lancaster. All across the city, de facto segregation provided African Americans with a daily reminder of their second-class status. The city had become a legal and cultural battleground for blacks and a few whites willing to challenge the dictates of those who refused to enforce Pennsylvania's desegregation laws. As people of color traveled into other parts of the city to shop at retail department stores, for leisure, or to look for jobs, the struggle for equality became a major axis of black–white confrontation. In the years leading up to the sixties, the effort to contain the black population in the Seventh Ward made Lancaster one of many northern cities beset by residential segregation and employment discrimination.

The fight against systemic racism in the city always kept African Americans energized. In the 1920s, when the black population was much smaller and activism against segregation was becoming more rigid—namely on account of the rhetorical battle between W. E. B. Du

Bois and Marcus Garvey—a branch of the National Association for the Advancement of Colored People, or NAACP, was formed inside the Bethel AME Church. On June 5, 1923, forty members, all African American, held the NAACP's first meeting.[1] As the decades passed, the branch evolved into a biracial organization that was a frontrunner for the direct nonviolent civil rights activism that came to define the grassroots movement leading up to James Meredith's March Against Fear. One of the most widely known popular legends involved the NAACP's takedown of the city's major department stores.

The effort to desegregate Lancaster's department stores was led by Rev. Alexander Stephans, pastor at the Bethel AME Church, and Kenneth K. Bost, president of the local NAACP. A controversial figure at the onset of his arrival in Lancaster, Bost heeded the message coming from the NAACP's national office in Chicago that encouraged local chapters to engage in "a summer of Negro discontent and public demonstration."[2] As long as the demonstration was nonviolent, the NAACP executives said, the form of public protests could be left up to local branches. Bost, accordingly, did not hesitate to employ Rev. Stephans to rally support within the community to launch a series of public protests.

The Bethel AME Church became the catalyst for bringing these issues to the surface. In July 1963, Bost and Stephans announced that the NAACP would launch a series of mass meetings to rally opposition against Lancaster's four largest downtown department stores: Watt & Shand, Hager & Bros., J. C. Penney, and Garvin's Department Store. The contention was that each of these four department stores refused to hire African American workers for meaningful jobs. "A couple of the downtown department stores had minorities working as elevator operators, but you could not go to the sales floor of any of those stores and buy something from a minority," recounts Gerald

Wilson, a Seventh Ward resident who marched with Stephans and Bost. "They just wouldn't hire them."[3]

The department stores, especially Watt & Shand, also had a reputation of refusing to serve black customers. "It was so humiliating," said Elizabeth Ford, a high school senior who marched with Stephans and Bost, "to go into those department stores, cash in hand, and [have them] refuse to serve us. If we wanted to buy something like a dress, a piece of clothing, the white salespeople would just stare us down. And heaven forbid if we would want to go and order lunch at their in-store lunch counter." Watt & Shand was the only department store in the city with a diner. Black patrons were allowed to order food from, but were not permitted to dine at, the establishment. "We would have to take the food out of the store," Ford said with indignation.[4]

The effort began when the NAACP's Freedom Committee sent a letter to eight major retail merchants, including Hager and Watt & Shand, "pointing out the urgent need to end racial discrimination in employment practices." The NAACP stated, "At the time of writing this letter, eight Negro young ladies had completed a distributive education course under the guidance of a qualified instructress and had applied for employment as salesgirls … None were hired."[5] They demanded two qualified African Americans be hired as sales clerks in each store.

On July 8, the NAACP reported that negotiations had begun between the chapter and representatives from the four department stores. Stephans and Bost were hoping that the meetings with the department store representatives would yield a negotiated agreement before any public demonstrations took place. J. C. Penney and Garvin's showed proof that they were already making efforts to hire African American employees.[6] Earlier that summer, J. C. Penney promoted a twenty-one-year-old African American woman named

Shirley Lucas from elevator operator to a retail sales position. In addition, both stores were already interviewing minority applicants for sales personnel.* Yet, Watt & Shand and Hager & Bros. assumed a position of discrimination. For that reason, Stephans and Bost called a general meeting at the Bethel AME Church on July 19 to energize the black populace and announce a demonstration against the two retail stores. "There has been talking, talking, talking for the last hundred years," Bost said. "It is time to stop talking. There have been applications and no results."

The NAACP demonstration included a nonviolent four-hour march in front of the two department stores and a boycott by the friends of NAACP members, who were urged not to purchase anything at either store until management could be persuaded to hire two black salespersons. Bost emphasized a "peaceful" march. "Let's not have any problems downtown," he demanded. Participants were informed that they might be called names, spat on, cursed at, or pushed. Ashley S. Dudley, chairman of the NAACP demonstration committee, suggested, "Someone may throw a brick at you but our purpose is not to fight back. Those of you who have a temper and can't take it had better stay away."[7]

The demonstration against the department stores began at ten o'clock in the morning on July 20. Marchers convened at the Bethel AME Church, where Rev. Stephans delivered a short sermon and prayer for the group. One marcher, Elizabeth Ford, remembers fifty

* Shirley Lucas (July 30, 1942–June 24, 2016) grew up at 464 Atlantic Avenue in Lancaster's Seventh Ward. She graduated from McCaskey High School in 1961, shortly thereafter obtaining a job as elevator operator at J. C. Penney. The job paid $1.25 per hour. Just before the start of the protests in 1963, Lucas believes her boss moved her into the sales department. She did not receive a pay increase. Lucas endured several interactions with white customers who refused to have her wait on them. She left J. C. Penney in 1964 to work at Hamilton Watch Company. She was the first African American to work in Hamilton's watch division.

years later Stephans' final caution: "This is God's work, not your work."[8] After the congregation sang religious songs and prayed, demonstrators carrying signs and American flags left the east side of Strawberry Street in double file and walked up South Queen Street toward Watt & Shand. At Mifflin Street, the marchers, now singing "We Shall Overcome," formed a single file line and walked closest to the Watt & Shand building, which the demonstration circled for one hour. The group then walked to Hager & Bros. in single formation and stood outside the store for another hour. Only a passing rain shower marred the peaceful protest. At one o'clock in the afternoon, a second shift of boycotters showed up to demonstrate outside of each store.

Though proud, participants were unsatisfied after that initial march. Two days later, 150 people marched again against Watt & Shand and Hager & Bros. Marchers walked single file along the Penn Square sidewalk in front of Watt & Shand for an hour and then moved to West King Street to demonstrate in front of Hager's. Kenneth Bost, wheeling his infant son in a stroller, led the parade. Marchers branded signs, some reading We Can Buy, Why Not Sell? and Hidden Prejudice Must Go. About twenty white demonstrators carried signs and flags with the group. Several of them were Franklin and Marshall College professors. "We did hurt them economically tonight," said Betty Tompkins, publicity chairwoman of the NAACP. "I didn't see many people going in and out of Watt & Shand and Hager's tonight, and that is what we want to see."[9] At the end of the march, Bost announced plans for a third demonstration against the department stores, this one set for Saturday, July 27, unless negotiations resulted in an agreement.

The boycott generated positive results. The evening after the second march, Thomas Shand, president of Watt & Shand, and John

R. Hager, spokesman for Hager's, indicated that they would attend a meeting on July 26 with Bost, members of the NAACP, and a representative from the mayor's office. Hager also indicated that his company had received its first application in "several years that day, from a Negro woman for a sales position[,] and the application is now being processed."[10] On Saturday morning, July 27, Bost canceled the planned march and announced that good-faith promises in hiring practices were made by the two department storeowners. The owners claimed that October 1 should give them ample time "to properly evaluate any applicants who may be forthcoming for jobs that open in our sales force." Since earlier meetings with the storeowners failed to produce similar outcomes, the NAACP accepted the proposal, "even though no commitment was made to hire a person by any certain date," claimed spokeswoman Betty Tompkins. Thomas Shand suggested the NAACP return in three weeks for an evaluation.

The fight for occupational opportunities in the city's department stores emerged as a galvanizing issue for Lancastrians in the summer of 1963. Things were changing. For the first time, whites in noticeable numbers, especially professors and students who were customarily vocal on college campuses, had taken an active role beside African Americans in community activism. For years, white liberals expressed sympathy, but now they were marching side by side with the black community. The momentum endured during the summer of 1963.

As was the case with many swimming pools across the country, racial segregation and discrimination at a few of Lancaster's private pools was nothing new. The managers of Maple Grove, Brookside, and Rocky Springs maintained segregated swimming pools. But the de facto discrimination at the Rocky Springs swimming pool was the most rigid of the trio.

The Rocky Springs Amusement Park was a major attraction for Lancastrians. On the surface, the amusement park brought together a heterogeneous mass into a racially cohesive crowd. Thousands every year jumped on the city's trolley and headed to Rocky Springs, where tourists were greeted by restaurants, thrilling rides, and sideshows designed to amuse guests. It boasted a carousel, a figure-eight roller coaster, a fun house, a Ferris wheel, airplane swings, bumper cars, a bowling alley, and a miniature train that was open to patrons of every race or color. However, inside of the amusement park was a swimming pool that was for whites only.

Nowhere in Lancaster was the symbol of segregation more prevalent than within Rocky Springs. One of the first documented cases of discrimination at Rocky Springs occurred on September 6, 1948, when its owner, Joseph Figari, kept two African American men, Edward A. Hudson and M. W. Richardson Jr., out of the pool during a company picnic. That year, plaintiffs brought suit against Figari, arguing that the commonwealth's Equal Rights Act of 1939 stated that owners of public accommodations, resorts, bathhouses, and amusement parks could not withhold their facilities "on account of race, creed, or color." Figari was convicted on the local level at the Lancaster County Courthouse. Thereafter, he lost his appeal to the Pennsylvania Supreme Court.

Nevertheless, segregation at the Rocky Springs swimming pool continued, as the court's decision was never enforced. The majority of the public allowed Figari and his pool manager, Toby Cathy, to maintain a segregated pool for two subsequent decades. This was especially apparent every summer when a gathering of several hundred African Americans from Chester and Lancaster Counties—most of them employed by Lukens Steel Company in Coatesville—met up at the annual Coatesville picnic at the Rocky Springs Amusement Park. "Every summer the amusement park's attractions were open for black people, but the pool always hung a sign on the entrance that said Closed for Repairs," remembers Coatesville picnic attendee Leroy Hopkins. "We all knew they closed the pool down during the picnic because a lot of black people were there."[11]

Figari and Cathy had lost in court, yet in the 1960s black Lancastrians like Hopkins were still forced to find other places to swim. That usually meant unsupervised adolescents and teenagers resorted to bathing in the creeks and rivers of Lancaster County. The locations were dangerous, especially since black children received no formal lessons and were swimming in waters with unpredictable depths. The popular bathing spot for black swimmers was a curvy section of the Conestoga Creek known as the Pogie, also known as the Poorhouse. The Pogie was a deep stretch of the creek that ran from the bottom of the hill where the site of the present-day Conestoga View Nursing Home is located on East King Street and the old Rocky Springs trolley bridge. Skillful Seventh Ward swimmers were drawn to the Pogie for its rope swing, which presented palpable dangers. Around 1910, one boy named Albert Brown died when he hit his head and drowned after jumping from the swing. Less experienced swimmers bathed at a stretch of the Conestoga River near the RCA tube plant called the Waterworks.[12]

The summer of 1963 brought new attention to Rocky Springs. In June, an African American looking to swim was turned away after he asked for an application to join the pool. Instead of saying outright that people of color were not welcome, Toby Cathy told the applicant, "Memberships are filled for this year."[13] The episode ignited a series of demonstrations arising from frustrations that had long been simmering among African Americans in the city.

In early July, while the NAACP was meeting with representatives from the downtown department stores, forty members of the local chapter met with Cathy and Figari to work out an agreement regarding Rocky Springs's record of discrimination. NAACP president Bost threatened a march on the amusement park if an agreement was not met. Despite high hopes, the encounter did not go very well.

At the end of July, Bost met with the members of the NAACP at their headquarters in the basement of the Bethel AME Church and announced his plan to conduct six marches during the month of August against Rocky Springs. However, he said that the demonstrations would be called off if Cathy could come to a satisfactory agreement with the Pennsylvania Human Relations Commission, which had stepped in as an arbitrator. The NAACP's demonstration chairman, Ashley Dudley, said, "The commission has been informed of our plans [and] is reviewing very many cases[,] so maybe this will cause the commission to move a little quicker on ours."[14]

Cathy appeared unthreatened. He mocked the Pennsylvania Human Relations Commission: "They [the Human Relations Commission] take them [accusations of injustice] around to places like Rocky Springs when the heat's put on by the colored outfit." Cathy said the demonstration against his pool would be a charade, because similar action was not planned against the managers at Maple Grove's and Brookside's swimming pools. Cathy's detractors at the NAACP responded cordially by affirming that the demonstrations would not be personal attacks. "He's already committed himself," said Dudley. "He's not going to let us in the pool."[15] Such thoughts were extraordinarily civil, but perhaps that was perfect for that time.

Once assembled, the NAACP announced its intention to march.

In a branch meeting on Wednesday, July 31, President Bost publicly reissued the call, telling potential marchers that they possessed the power necessary to generate change that would impact the entire community. Over 150 marchers were expected to take part in the first weekend of marches. The staging point for each of the demonstrations was the Bethel AME Church, from where they would caravan to the Rocky Springs Amusement Park, located almost two miles northeast, through the Seventh Ward. From the parking lot, demonstrators would circle the pool before heading back to the church.

So on the third day of August, from his base at the Bethel AME Church, Bost's first march departed for Rocky Springs. Eighty-seven people, including a dozen white marchers, walked in orderly fashion one by one to the city's pool. After arriving at Rocky Springs, the demonstrators approached the pool's entrance, turned left, and marched along the perimeter of the fence. Inside of the pool were several dozen distraught white children, their parents, and Cathy, who peered out at the demonstration. Some in the pool splashed the marchers, who accepted it as a blessing. "That was great," one marcher declared.[16] It was close to 100 degrees that day.

All in all, the demonstration was peaceful. But that evening, vandals used white paint to graffiti the acronym KKK, six inches high, on several parts of the Bethel AME Church.[17] Early the next morning, Stephans and Bost met with the community to relate the incident. The men were both deeply shocked. Stephans later told a reporter that he felt the marks "could be symbols of something perhaps pettiness, narrowness or shortsightedness on the part of those who did it."[18] The vandalism, in no way, was going to interfere with the boycott. Rev. Stephans said that conducting the march that day as planned was the only way forward. Anything less than this would not get the message across to Cathy and other segregationists.

That afternoon, sixty black and white demonstrators carrying small American flags and signs showed up for Bost's second demonstration. The placards announced, "We're walking for our rights," "Our color won't wash off," "We feel the heat, too," and "Prejudice handicaps our nation." About one hundred adults and children watched the march from inside the pool. There were more onlookers outside of the pool sitting on park benches and picnic tables. The pool's public address system played rock-and-roll music in an attempt to drown out the picketers. Rather, the demonstrators marched to "You've Got to Walk That Lonesome Valley" and "Move Your Feet." A newspaper reported, "The lyrics of the music brought smiles to the faces of a number of the walkers." Bost cried out, "Look at that swimming pool. Look at the people in it. How would you feel if you were standing out here with a flag on your shoulder and your child couldn't go in?"

Bost, a seasoned campaigner for racial justice, was fully aware of the consequences of his nonviolent yet radical action, knowing well of earlier struggles. A thirty-nine-year old tailor, Bost initially had been a member of the NAACP in Philadelphia before moving to Lancaster in 1955. That year, he became interested in radical efforts after a real estate agent told him "that he could not buy a home on Christian Street because he was a Negro."[19] He was highly revered by many in the Seventh Ward because of his service during World War II. Bost was a member of the 503rd Anti-Aircraft Battalion stationed at the Maui Island Airport in the Pacific theater during World War II. He was promoted from radio operator to communications chief as a sergeant in charge of all communications. His unit went in as part of the Okinawa invasion on June 6, 1945. After the raid, Bost was promoted to fire control electrician. "The last two enemy aircraft shot down during World War II in the Pacific were hit by my battery and our sister battery," Bost bragged. That resiliency learned in the Second World War was the trait he tried to teach his followers in Lancaster. The marches outside the Rocky Springs swimming pool made him the movement's engine. He was blessed with a temperament that was unsullied and that exhibited entrenched devotion to the people who followed.

The next march, on Saturday, August 11, gained more attention. Seventh Warder Herbert A. Cooper called it "a public protest to let citizens know that we do not have equal opportunity." The march, with forty-seven participants when it left the Bethel AME Church, grew to consist of nearly a hundred demonstrators as the procession made its way to Rocky Springs. "People just join us and fall in line," Cooper explained. Two of the marchers were young men who lived in the Seventh Ward: Leroy Hopkins, a junior linguistics major at Millersville State College, and Chet Stewart, a playground supervisor at Rockland and Green Playground. "I just feel," Hopkins said, "that it is a sort of challenge to me to do the best I can for the movement, the main goal of which is equal opportunity for all." Hopkins, who became a well-respected professor of German at Millersville University, admitted that he never learned to swim. He earned Ds in his high school swim classes while a student at J. P. McCaskey High School, where all of the male students were forced to swim, not only in integrated waters but also naked. The low grades in swim class kept him off the honor roll. But at this moment, he admitted that he was marching "for others." Stewart, meanwhile, explained how the demonstrations against Rocky Springs woke up the young people of the Seventh Ward. "They want to prove themselves," Stewart said.[20]

The NAACP's marches around Rocky Springs failed to yield the same result that the department store boycott had produced. Chief among the reasons was that Bost's marches did not place anxiety related to finances upon the pool's owner like the boycott against the retailers had. Cathy was still determined to keep black swimmers out of his pool a year later when President Lyndon Johnson signed the Civil Rights Act into law, guaranteeing all citizens, regardless of race, equal protection of the law under the Fourteenth Amendment. When the NAACP's efforts to desegregate the pool made enough progress in the city, Cathy smugly proclaimed that he would rather close his pool and fill it in with dirt than be forced to open it up to black swimmers.* Years later Cathy closed his pool. "Oh yeah," remembers J. Donald Schaeffer, a twenty-five-year police officer who walked the beat in the Seventh Ward during the sixties, in 1966 "[Cathy] filled it in with dirt and planted a garden."[21]

The demonstrations in Lancaster, a city in a northern state, occurred at a poignant time during Martin Luther King's nonviolent struggle against the Jim Crow system. A month before Bost's boycott and before marches brought attention to the issues afflicting Lancaster, thousands of children marching to desegregate Birmingham, Alabama, found themselves in prison or attacked with fire hoses and police dogs. A few months later, members of Ku Klux Klan bombed the 16th Street Baptist Church where those marches had begun. Four young girls between the ages of eleven and fourteen were killed, while a fifth child, a sister of one of the deceased victims, was blinded in one eye. These actions did not occur in vain, as the Civil Rights Act was passed in 1964, delivering the deathblow to legal segregation across the South. One year later, after thousands more marched from Selma to Montgomery, the Voting Rights Act wedged a final stake into Jim Crow when it permitted federal agents the right to

---

* The first integrated public swimming pool, Conestoga Pines, opened in August 1966 at the site of the Waterworks property. In 1967, the Lancaster County Public Swimming Pool opened at Lancaster County Park.

ensure equal voting practices in states that had historically prohibited African Americans from voting.

These legal victories did not mean the end of segregation. The fact remained that although America's discrimination laws were eliminated, residential segregation, poverty, and other systemic forms of discrimination still permeated American society after 1965. Owing to these experiences of being black in the United States there arose another tide. Several people in the Seventh Ward would have a different name for it: black power.

Chapter 3

THE DISCONTENT

<hr />

IF ANYONE NEEDED a reminder that there would be more difficult times ahead, Benjamin Bethea was the person to provide it. Bethea's inevitable participation in the local black power movement stems all the way back to his childhood. An impulsive boy, he was born in Brooklyn, where there was upward mobility of African Americans as lawyers and teachers. Bethea, by reason of his auspicious childhood and his reputation for being a precocious youth, gained a practical education through his early life encounters. Every summer his parents would take him to visit relatives in North Carolina, where his aunts and uncles were sharecroppers. As a child, he labored with them in the field, harvesting tobacco, a labor-intensive task that included chopping and stringing the crop. The young Benjamin joined his uncles picking cotton, tomatoes, and watermelons. "They just worked," he anguished, "but I would never see money change [hands]." The business transactions between tenant farmers and his relatives were abusive in Bethea's opinion. "The white man would give them a little plot of land that they could crop themselves, but they never got paid cash," Bethea objected. He continued, "It was, 'You can do this for me, but take a couple crumbs for yourself.' And I didn't like that." It depressed him to visit his cousins and see them struggle to earn enough for a decent meal.

Bethea's experiences in North Carolina were not isolated to the field. His most vivid memory of the South was his experience dealing with Jim Crow in Union County. He remembered being chased out of a whites-only billiard room by a group of men. Unfamiliar with the social reality under the culture of Jim Crow, Bethea wanted to show his cousins how brave he was, so he walked into the pool hall and sat down. "Black bastard," those in the pool hall yelled. "Black nigger, what are you doing in here!" Bethea realized the trouble he was in and took off running. When he arrived home, he received a thrashing from his father. He admitted that there was a message in the reprimand: "[My dad] was trying to tell me to realize where I was at." It was a point all too relevant in the African American community during the mid-1950s, as only years before Emmett Till, a Chicagoan by birth, had been killed at the hands of Mississippians for not understanding the culture of a place subjugated by the Jim Crow system.* Bethea was deeply disturbed by those experiences. "I was a child, and [my] vengeance grew." He told himself, "When I grow up,

---

* Emmett Till was fourteen years old on August 24, 1955, when he visited a local store run by Roy and Carolyn Bryant in Money, Mississippi. He was known for bragging to his cousins and friends in Mississippi about having white girlfriends back home in Chicago. That day, something happened inside Bryant's Grocery and Meat Market that upset Mrs. Bryant, who stormed out of the store after Till, presumably to grab a gun from her car. Till was rushed away from the scene by his friends after he whistled to her as she headed to her parked car. Four days later, around 2:30 in the morning, Roy Bryant and his half brother, J. W. Milam, pounded on the door of Mose Wright, Till's great-uncle, and demanded to see Till. After forcing their way in, Bryant and Milam abducted Till. The teenager's disfigured body was discovered three days later in the Tallahatchie River. Despite the family ring on Till's finger, an all-white, all-male jury acquitted Bryant and Milam, claiming there was insufficient evidence proving that it was, in fact, Till's body.

I'm going to get these people back." Although the movement had yet to be called *black power*, it was in the 1950s when Bethea discovered the tenuousness of standing with a revolutionary movement. In the South, "[Whites] didn't even want our money." As an adolescent boy from Brooklyn, Bethea learned that in the South, "Blacks had their own gas stations, their own pharmacy, [and] their own funeral homes." For a time, he "thought that was better [than] when someone tells you face-to-face that 'I don't like you.'" Shocked and dismayed by the distinction of visiting the South, Bethea saw a dramatic contrast with his life in the North. "They [northerners] would say, 'We don't mind that you give us your money, but we don't want you messing with our daughters or things like that.'"[1]

Tall in stature, and convincing in speech and walk, Bethea's dark-skinned stocky body bore countless scars. From his preacher father, he inherited a round nose, thick eyebrows, a solid chin, and fingers that could tickle piano keys like no other. Many considered Bethea a prodigy pianist. It was a skill he developed while attending his father's Pentecostal church that he so despised. Bethea was a natural leader who prided himself on his vision, but of late he had found his anger increasingly hard to check. He had come to enjoy being revolutionary.

The Bethea family moved to Lancaster in 1962. Benjamin's aunt, who was a cofounder of the Pentecostal church on Rockland and Green Streets, was the first in the family to arrive in the Seventh Ward. His father chose to move Ben; his three brothers, Godfrey, Gerald, and Alfred; and his three sisters, Sylvia, Evelyn, and Jennifer, to Lancaster so he could pastor for her church: the Church of Deliverance for All Nations. The Betheas moved into a house on Green Street, across the road from the church. Bethea was always angry with his father. "We went from being lower middle class in New York to being poverty-stricken here [in Lancaster]," he objected. As a teenager, he worked on nearby Amish farms picking collard greens and berries, and killing groundhogs for his family to eat. "I hated that stuff," he said indignantly.

Bethea grew restless at his new home. Friends later remarked on his deep-seated anger, saying that he had a forward tilt as if ready to wade into a brawl at any moment. While the Edward Hand Junior High sat on the edge of the neighborhood, African American students from the Seventh Ward had to travel through the city's white areas to get to the high school. At the northeastern edge of the city is J. P. McCaskey High School, a beautiful example of 1930s architecture constructed by workers employed by President Roosevelt's Works Progress Administration. Bethea explained that black high school students usually "traveled in packs." But one day after school in 1967, his sister Jennifer walked home alone and was mugged by a group of white teenagers. Outraged, he prepared himself to defend his sister. The next day, heart pounding and pistol in hand, Bethea, who had been expelled from the high school three years earlier, showed up at McCaskey fully intent on making a statement. He claimed to have fired shots outside the school and then to have fled the scene. No one was harmed, and Bethea avoided arrest.

After the incident, the youthful stain of criminality in Bethea's character hardened into something dark. He had been lucky to escape apprehension after unloading his weapon outside the school. Something internal, however, made him numb and extremely bitter. He admitted, "My perception was that I was always being hurt by a particular group of people, and I always told myself that I was going to hurt them whenever I got old enough and big enough and bad enough." Looking back on his actions in later years, Bethea acknowledged that there was a time in his life when he "got relief from hurting" others. He expressed genuine remorse before he passed away in 2013. "I told strangers, as long as they were white, I'd get ya." He recanted, saying, "That's the part I'm ashamed of ... Most everything I did was a sin."[2]

These were radicalizing experiences that caused Bethea to become an activist with revolutionary objectives. With other Seventh Warders like Robert Boyer and Russell Bair, Bethea was driven by ambition to offer more to the movement than most people. In the final months of 1967, an unofficial chapter of the Black Panther Party was formed spontaneously in Lancaster. "We called ourselves panthers," Bethea divulged, "but we split from the [Black] Panthers because we felt that they were too nonviolent." Instead, Bethea's group called itself Black Arise. The group took its name from its motto: "When the black from their sleep arise, then the black shall be free!"*

Free from the dictates of the national Black Panther Party, Black Arise developed aggressive strategies against the racist power structure in Lancaster. "It is the power structure who are the pigs and hogs who have been robbing the people," wrote Bobby Seale in his book *Seize the Time* (1970). "We see [the Black Panther Party] as a necessity for us to progress as human beings and live on the face of this earth along with other people."[3] Seale's austere message, and Black Panther cofounder Huey Newton's unbending faith in liberating the black race, yielded a fierce following in Lancaster. According to those who supported Black Arise, revolutionary violence was necessary. "We practice non-violence and will stay non-violent except when the white man becomes violent or tries to stop our struggle for freedom," explained Black Arise cofounder Robert Boyer. "Then, we feel at this point, we must become violent."[4] Though counter to the original

---

* Robert Boyer, a 1966 graduate of J. P. McCaskey High School, was a cross-country and distance track-and-field runner. He sang with a choir called the Gospel Monarchs before and while he was a Black Arise member.

intent of the Black Panther Party, Boyer and Bethea's concept of violence helped develop their chapter's reputation.

Black Arise, a relative of the Black Panther Party, swaggered through the second half of the sixties recruiting members and disseminating messages about employment, housing, education, and inequity in the criminal justice system. The party touted Second Amendment rights, arguing that people of color had the right to use guns to defend themselves against attacks from white ruffians and to repel police brutality.[5] This was the divisive issue in the black empowerment debate. Some admired the idea of armed defense. Others found those tactics too aggressive, believing that they could possibly lead to heightened harassment from the police force or the recoil of the civil rights movement's major accomplishments. Still, the Black Arise Party in Lancaster adhered to the message of armed defense.

Imitating the methods of the Black Panthers as shown on television and in Panther literature, Black Arise flaunted an abrasive yet hip urban attitude. Wearing black leather jackets, berets, and turtlenecks, Black Arise members set out to recruit anyone who was black into their organization. The first recruitment meeting was held inside the Higbee Elementary School in September 1967. The meeting was well attended by Seventh Ward residents and college students from Franklin and Marshall and Millersville State. Bethea spent days before the meeting hanging signs and passing out flyers, which made community members very curious. Ramilee Brown, a twenty-four-year-old Seventh Warder who attended the meeting, was immediately turned off by the revolutionary rhetoric coming from the meeting's organizers. "I heard such hatred from people, and I said to myself, 'Oh my God, I won't be coming back here again,'" remembers Brown. People fussed over how to handle the revolution, and Bethea attempted to teach the listeners how to prepare. "He was telling us … how to put your BM—bowel movement—into jars and let it sit for a month or so, then dip safety pins and pens in it. Then [we were instructed to] throw it on people[,] and that would cause bad illness or some kind of disease."[6] That message was enough to turn Brown away.*

But Bethea and the founding members of Black Arise kept attempting to establish a foothold in the Seventh Ward. They recruited between thirty and forty members after the first meeting. "Maybe two males to every female," Bethea said. Nobody in the organization was over the age of twenty-five. "We got involved with college students," Bethea revealed, "black ones from Millersville and mostly F&M." Together with Seventh Ward residents, Black Arise members would eventually form the nucleus of the organization's intelligence ministry. The range of members allowed the organization to get a broad view of what was going on throughout Lancaster County.

Structurally, Black Arise appeared to be evenly organized, much like the Black Panther Party. It possessed centralized leadership and had party rules. It encouraged Seventh Ward youths to get involved in community survival programs by volunteering at the neighborhood's only doctor's office, barbershop, and day care center. It attempted to tackle Lancaster's poverty problems by incorporating a free breakfast program into its daily activities. "It was a huge problem," Bethea said, speaking of the poverty in his neighborhood. Black Arise's free breakfast program was one of its biggest successes. "We provided free and healthy breakfasts for kids who needed it," Bethea avowed. The Black Panther Party had provided guidelines for local organizations

* Ramilee Brown (b. 1943) is a lifelong resident of the Seventh Ward. She grew up on Atlantic Avenue and was a supporter of Malcolm X's aggressive position. Although she attended the inaugural meeting, she renounced Black Arise.

like Black Arise to carry out social revitalization programs. Details included daily menus of eggs, grits, ham, bacon, and toast. The free breakfast program was a lifesaver, as most families in the ward struggled to make ends meet.

While the redevelopment projects of the sixties were intended to desegregate the Seventh Ward, Black Arise members graded them a failure. Party members contended that the demolition blighted the ward further. Bethea explained, "Buildings were torn down even as few project buildings were put up." The people, meanwhile, remained in the area. Ward residents were homeowners before the renovation projects, but afterward they had become renters. By 1967, Lancaster had become the sixth most densely populated city in the United States.[7] It was an unfortunate consequence resulting from the attempt to create a more heterogeneous Lancaster. While there existed veteran Seventh Warders who possessed a sense of trust of and accountability to one another, the younger, more radical Black Arise members insisted on their type of change.

Pragmatically, Black Arise did not understand how to build prosperity. The party's intentions for the community were earnest, but poor economic circumstances in the Seventh Ward combined with the decision to operate free from the oversight of the Oakland chapter of the Black Panther Party gave rise to a criminal element among its members. Black Arise did not investigate the backgrounds of its recruits. Many unchecked members quickly became opportunistic, engaging in petty criminal activities that became both a misrepresentation of and stain on Black Arise, the latter of which could not be wiped clean. Much of the illegal misconduct derived from the violence witnessed in the Vietnam War. Black Arise's criminality was rationalized by some members who misguidedly pointed to the example set by the US government that maimed and killed hundreds of thousands of Vietnamese people and presented itself as a contradiction of American ideals of self-determination and justice. The group was responsible for firebombing the selective service center in hopes of destroying draft records. Black Arise was also accountable for bombing the offices of various landlords in the Seventh Ward with the intent of destroying rent records.[8]

That was revolutionary work for Black Arise in the late sixties. In the eyes of society at large, however, members of Black Arise were thugs and crooks. Local lore suggests they robbed banks and white-owned supermarkets. Members conducted synchronized robberies: they stole food and money from several grocery stores scattered throughout the city in order to redistribute it among the community's needy citizens.

Benjamin Bethea tried to justify their actions by saying that Black Arise worked for those who were being discounted by Lancaster's power elite. "There were people working at RCA or Armstrong who couldn't read or write, but they had jobs [and] they were all white," Bethea said with indignation. He argued that many in his neighborhood struggled to find work other than what he described as "service jobs, low menial service jobs." The few positions available for African Americans outside the Seventh Ward were on chicken farms. "It was nasty," Bethea emphasized. "They would load us on trucks and take us to Bird-in-Hand," far outside of the city. "The only other jobs were janitorial or cleaning people's houses," he added. It all helped turn "us mad."[9]

Bethea was a central authority under Black Arise's executive leadership. He served as the party's minister of defense. It was a role that found him supervising his own neighborhood and protecting black residents from encounters with the police. "We policed our own community," Bethea said. "We had a structure." He pointed out, "We worked out of a building [in the Seventh Ward]."[10] The headquarters, located at 429 Green Street, functioned as the organization's academy, dormitory, situation room, and weapons depot. The opening of the Green Street headquarters was not a clandestine operation. Some of Black Arise's members listed that address as their primary place of residence. Black Arise members walked in and out of the house in broad daylight. Not exactly a safe haven, the Green Street house was left alone by the law enforcers.

Black Arise tried in earnest to create an educational system that evaluated the position of black people in the world. The organization assessed Gandhi's and Martin Luther King's nonviolent methods, and compared those to the doctrines of black nationalism taught by Marcus Garvey and Malcolm X. Bethea confessed, "We liked literary types." Yet, Black Arise members gravitated toward socialism, believing that capitalism kept minorities oppressed. To those in Black Arise, persons of African descent in the United States were a colonized people dominated by a power that shared the land within the USA's borders. The physical distance between mother country and the colonized people was not the issue here. Rather, the gap in education, the assault on the conscious, the difference in wealth status, and the discrepancy in the rate of incarceration amounted to a domestic form of colonialism. The objective of every activist in the black liberation struggle was to create a society without exploiters and exploited persons. They worked to form an ideal socioeconomic state where every person could give to the society according to his or her ability and talents, and that person in turn could receive materials in accordance with his or her needs. If that ideal state could not be achieved peacefully, Bethea and other Black Arise members felt, then armed insurrection was their only option. "We studied Mao Zedong," explained Bethea. Party members read and discussed

Mao's *Little Red Book*. By educating and arming those in Lancaster's black community, and by teaching them to live revolutionary lives, Black Arise could ready the people to contribute to the looming socialist revolution. Perhaps the members of Black Arise were in over their heads, especially by concentrating on the irrelevant leader of the Peoples Republic of China, yet Bethea's account of the type of meetings he had with fellow members seems both astute and credible: "We met pretty frequently and did our homework. Then [we'd] have sessions about black awareness. We'd talk about the Middle Passage, and Frederick Douglass's writing, and Du Bois versus Booker T. Washington."[11]

Bethea and confidant Robert Boyer forged intimate bonds with people whom they considered intellectual companions. The two men bought into Black Panther founder Huey P. Newton's "black school of thought," a string of values centered on black liberation. Bethea said, "Freedom for everybody or freedom for nobody." This notion emphasized racial self-determination, simultaneously emphasizing cultural awareness and racial separation. Bethea and Boyer wanted people of their race to be called "Black" or "Afro-American." The term *Negro* was antiquated, even humiliating. Black Arise's minister of interior, responsible for recruiting members, was Boyer, who said that the term "*Negro* is made up of two parts—*ne*, meaning 'never,' and *gro*, meaning 'grow.'" He explained, "'Never grow'—it means nothing." He said that even after the major civil rights legislation was passed in Congress, there would never be integration on a full scale. "The system is set up in the interests of the majority[,] and the majority is white … Black people today are thinking of having their own government and black nation."[12] Accordingly, Black Arise made the Seventh Ward its own jurisdiction.

It was vital to impart the message about a black government and a black nation to the area's young people. "We realize most older folks everywhere have more patience[,] and it is no different with the black older generation. They are conditioned to accept conditions as they are. But black youths," Boyer contended, "are determined to make necessary changes now." Black Arise leaders worked with students from the city's high school and the Seventh Ward's only middle school, Edward Hand Junior High. Its educational philosophy included a commitment to the arts, as black students were taught to put on skits and plays about their heritage. Black Arise members wished to see young black students, as Boyer described, "prepare themselves to set up businesses in the black community after graduation from high school or college."[13] They further saw that white guidance counselors often ignored or failed to understand the problems of black youths. Accordingly, Black Arise established a guidance committee to work with its Seventh Ward students. Boyer said, "We would work with black students who we feel are not getting proper guidance through white guidance counselors, and follow their progress throughout the year, from junior high through high school." They wanted Seventh Ward students to bring their school problems to them "without fear of incriminating themselves." The Black Arise Guidance Committee functioned as an intermediary that would listen to students' problems and then present the grievances to the proper school authorities. In essence, the group filled the "communications gap" that existed among teachers, students, and parents.

Convinced that they had no alternative, Boyer and Bethea rallied the community to establish a legal defense coalition between Black Arise and the city's Community Action Program. It was called the Black People's Defense League. The men claimed that public defenders often failed to provide African Americans adequate representation. In addition, they perceived that excessive bail was often set for African Americans who had been arrested. In Lancaster, there were "two systems of justice," contended Boyer, "one for the white and one for the black."[14] Supporters of the Defense League did not want to depend on public defenders. Meanwhile, the men were cognizant of the lofty price of an attorney, so they sought help from the Community Action Program to fund their own defense team.

Russell Bair, known in Seventh Ward circles as Larry, was probably the most active Black Arise member at the group's inception in 1967. He was a thin man weighing no more than 160 pounds, had a sharply curved chin, a round nose, a high sloping forehead, thin eyebrows, and an Afro. In one capacity, Bair was the vice president of the Black Leopard Boxing Club, which was partially funded by Black Arise. Bair spent much of his time developing the physical appearance of Seventh Ward youths. He also encouraged young men and women to wear African-type clothing. He said girls in home economics classes ought to be taught how to make dashikis, head wraps, *agbadas*, and other African clothing.

Party members took what they learned from their discussions at 429 Green Street and disseminated those messages to people in other cities. Bethea explains, "We then branched out and went to other cities," namely, Pittsburgh, Detroit, and Chicago. He said Black Arise established a network with members of the Revolutionary Action Movement in Philadelphia and had "black power conferences and workshops" in other parts of the country.[15]

Not quite a political and social juggernaut with about thirty members, Black Arise's attitude of black power entrenched itself in one Lancaster County campus where belief turned into profession. The intellectual component of black liberation reached Franklin and Marshall College (also referred to as F&M) only months after the formation of the Black Panther Party and its auxiliary Black Arise. Though Franklin and Marshall is a long way physically from Oakland, the fury of its black student community when it came to establishing black educational programs on campus had everything to do with the social movement that was already challenging white authority throughout the United States. The exclusion of black curriculum and black faculty, in addition to the company of only a small number of black peers in a white domain on the college campus, kept white students ignorant of black social realities and deprived black students of their cultural development.[16]

Chapter 4

THE AFRO-AMERICAN SOCIETY

IN MANY RESPECTS, Franklin and Marshall College should be credited for making concerted efforts to recruit African American students from various high schools along the East Coast of the United States. Long before it was in vogue, the admissions office sent representatives to travel throughout the North and South recruiting minority students from cities like New York, New Haven, District of Columbia, Baltimore, Greensboro, and Tallahassee. Franklin and Marshall's signature outreach was a summer program that offered special experiences to disadvantaged youngsters who had the potential to succeed in college. The program was called the Pre-College Enrichment Program (PREP). The idea for PREP developed in 1963 when Franklin and Marshall president Keith Spalding appointed a special ad hoc committee responsible for examining how the college could provide educational opportunities for culturally disadvantaged urban students. The committee was eventually named the Committee on Inter-Racial Affairs. It determined that the major problem facing black students was the "inequality of pre-college education" created and fostered by segregated schools.[1] The committee concluded that a large number of black students aspiring to higher education were inadequately prepared for college. Additionally, the committee concluded, black students were scoring deficiently in reading, writing, and verbal skills, thus leading them to "do rather badly, particularly in their first year" of college.[2] The idea for PREP sprung from these statistics. Its founders wanted to create a program for underachieving students whose grades were lower than their ability.

During the 1963–1964 academic year, Franklin and Marshall College received a onetime grant of $40,000 from New York investment banker David Rockefeller. That year, other groups and philanthropists donated an additional $15,000 to launch the PREP experiment.[3] Arrangements were then made to enroll fifty-four black men and one white pupil into F&M's inaugural PREP summer program. Four cooperating institutions, Cheyney State College, Delaware State College, Morgan State College, and Lincoln University, selected forty-three students from their entering freshman classes, and Franklin and Marshall recommended twelve students. Under the directorship of English professor Gerald Enscoe, the program ran during an eight-week period from June 29 to August 22, 1964.[4]

Many hoped that PREP, with a few adjustments, would be maintained as a regular part of the college's summer activities. Since the program carried significant financial demands, which included books, instruction, room, board, and a $300 scholarship per student, the Committee on Inter-Racial Affairs fretted over the chances of sustaining PREP for even one more summer. Fortunately, when Rockefeller's grant expired in 1965, the college received special funding from the National Scholarship Service and Fund for Negro Students as long as PREP accepted nineteen high school seniors from Hattiesburg, Mississippi. As a result, PREP carried on its residential program for a second summer. Fellow "Prepsters" eventually dubbed the southerners "the Mississippi 19."[5]

The summer of 1965 was particularly interesting for the Mississippi 19, who were given the opportunity to interact with Lancaster City's Seventh Ward residents. A white Franklin and Marshall student, Leslie Lenkowsky, inaugurated the Lancaster Community Day Camp for students of junior high age (i.e., grades 7–9) who lived in the Seventh Ward. The city's swimming pools were still segregated in 1965. Disturbed by this, Lenkowsky, originally from Connecticut, approached college administrators about creating an opportunity for Seventh Ward residents to swim at Franklin and Marshall's pool three days a week. Lenkowsky was an exceptional student at Franklin and Marshall. He was a featured reporter for the *College Reporter*, special affairs director for the college's radio station WWFM, coeditor of Franklin and Marshall literary magazine *The Prologue*, and chairman of the Committee for Social Change. For a time, he worked as assistant director of PREP. Lenkowsky had been a cofounder of the Student War on Poverty, or SWOP, which allowed Franklin and Marshall's students, mostly black, to tutor and mentor children living with financial and personal difficulties in the Seventh Ward.* His involvement in that organization made it possible for him

---

* The Student War on Poverty Program (SWOP) was founded in the fall of 1965 by Leslie Lenkowsky and other F&M students who worked in a street-corner day camp in Lancaster during the summer of 1964. The program was designed to help young students from very poor, broken, or disturbed homes in the city and/or county. The tutoring program targeted ten- to fifteen-year-old students. Instructors were predominantly African American. Lenkowsky had come to F&M from Connecticut. After learning about Lancaster's segregated swimming pools, he started a program that allowed the city's black children to use the pool at F&M. That program evolved into SWOP, which enabled Lancaster's youths to attend F&M sporting events for free. The tutorial program was to help first-through-sixth-graders in reading. SWOP included a Big Brother program that sent mentors to work five hours a week with a youngster.

to become acquainted with the troubles of Lancaster's black residents, nearly all of whom lived in the Seventh Ward.[6] He indeed obtained approval from the board of trustees and the consent of President Keith Spalding to manage a program that enabled city youngsters to use the college's pool three times a week during summer break.[7] The combination of black Mississippians interacting with black Pennsylvanians created a positive and educational atmosphere for first-time visitors to rural Lancaster County.

To retain the program for a third summer in 1966, Franklin and Marshall received a financial boost from alumni, trustees, churches, and friends of the college. Also, the federal Office of Economic Opportunity, as part of President Lyndon Johnson's War on Poverty, was operating a program called Upward Bound. The Office of Special Programs applied for and received funds from the Upward Bound program, which kept PREP operational for another decade.[8] The college's healthy academic environment facilitated a high degree of value for its Prepsters. "We hoped that we would discover youngsters who never suspected that they possessed talent," indicated Dick Schneider, who served as one of PREP's directors.

As of 1966, PREP evolved into a three-year commitment for aspiring collegians from central Pennsylvania, largely coming from Harrisburg, Lancaster, York, Reading, and Red Lion. The program was designed for high school sophomores, juniors, and seniors. A student entered the program during the summer between his or her sophomore and junior year. Graduation from PREP was set for the end of the summer following a student's high school graduation. On any given PREP weekend at Franklin and Marshall, up to sixty college-bound students spent several weeks on campus attending various classes and seminar programs. Specifically, PREP remediated skills in reading, writing, personal confidence, and public speaking by enrolling its students in English, mathematics, and art classes. Professors from each respective department taught the classes. Student tutors were hired to nurture the learning process after classroom hours. Classroom conditions were the same as those students in college would find. Extracurricular activities reflected those of a typical college semester, including providing Prepsters the opportunity to publish a newspaper, operate a radio station, play in a band, act in theater, hear visiting lecturers, take weekend field trips, play intramural sports, and attend the church, synagogue, or mosque of each student's choice.

The director of Franklin and Marshall's Office of Special Programs, the campus organization that managed PREP, was Pauline Leet, an English professor who became PREP's administrator in 1965. She subsequently became PREP's most revered advocate before the time she resigned in 1968. By way of Connecticut, Leet arrived in Lancaster in 1963 when her husband, Albert, obtained a job at Franklin and Marshall teaching English. A mother of one boy and pregnant with another when she and Albert arrived, Leet was not involved with PREP during the program's inaugural summer. She joined up with the college during the spring of 1965 as the Office of Special Program's organizer and fixer. Her first job was to work with the Mississippi 19. As director of PREP, she was a doer. Slender, passionate, and intelligent, with long hair often worn in a braid and a quaint sense of humor, Leet was a capable fund-raiser who hounded local churches and corporations for donations. She possessed an irreplaceable gift for relating to the PREP students, and her compassion stretched well beyond the few weeks she spent with them each summer. During the fall and spring semesters, she created study centers in York, Harrisburg, and Lancaster. Leet hired adults in each city to facilitate the study centers, and paid college students, who were normally her PREP tutors, to travel to each site to instruct the Prepsters. Normally, she mailed paperback novels to each PREP student, and once a month brought the Prepsters back to Franklin and Marshall for book discussions and movies.

Leet developed a unique relationship with the Mississippi 19. During Thanksgiving break in 1965, she traveled to Mississippi to spend the holiday with the students. While there, she had valid concerns about the safety of her own life while being chauffeured around the state by a black woman and in the company of black men. She had arrived in Mississippi only one year after the violence of the Freedom Summer. After arriving at the airport, she spent the next three days with her PREP students. Presenting the image of a confident white woman chumming around with several black men opened her up to many stares and insults.[9] In spite of that, Leet and each one of the Mississippi 19 spent a memorable weekend together.

Leet's students venerated her. Everyone saw her as a passionate role model who invested all of her energy in the program. "I sometimes wonder which one of her three kids Mrs. Leet likes the most," said Prepster Marcia Sternbergh, "Joshua, Matthew, or PREP." Much of the students' admiration was due to Leet's sincere concern for their welfare. "I believed completely, and so did many others, in what we were doing," Leet recalled in an interview three decades after her resignation from PREP. "When a group of new kids came in, I'd give each kid in the program a dime and I'd say, 'Call me if you get any crap. Call me if anyone says you're not college material.' They'd call me and I would go to their homes or to their high schools. I was young with lots of energy, and I felt I was doing the Lord's work."[10]

Leet found unique ways to keep the Prepsters coming back every summer. In 1965, her first year directing PREP, she called up a politically connected Franklin and Marshall alumnus and future White House chief of staff to Ronald Reagan named Kenneth Duberstein and convinced him to sponsor a trip to the New York World's Fair in Flushing Meadows' Corona Park. She also planned a field trip to Washington, DC, where PREP students enjoyed a planned encounter with US Senator Robert F. Kennedy. "This little skinny guy walks in [a Senate caucus room], the saddest human being I had ever seen," Leet recollected. "He shook hands with every student before he left."[11] Leet took her students to the Baltimore Colts' training camp and to Philadelphia Phillies games. In 1967, Sargent Shriver visited Franklin and Marshall to praise her and PREP's mission.

The students were so moved by Leet's commitment that the dedication in the 1967 *Prepster Yearbook* was devoted to her. It read, "You're an angel, Mrs. Leet. That's the only word we know."[12]

Grudgingly, Leet resigned from PREP after the 1968 summer program when she was accepted into the Harvard Graduate School of Education. "I had fallen in love with the program," she confessed many years after her retirement from Franklin and Marshall. "These were exceptional kids. We had a fantastic time together."[13]

As she neared the end of her tenure, Leet had time to prepare her most trusted tutor for life after college. A sociology major from Chambersburg, Pennsylvania, named Lewis H. Myers was Leet's legacy. An employee of PREP from 1966 to 1968, Myers was one of the most vocal and involved African American students on campus. A member of the Class of 1968, Myers's own ambition helped the high school Prepsters reinvent themselves during their short stay on campus. The son of an AME Zion preacher, Myers had arrived on campus from a predominantly white high school in Franklin County. He had been the president of his high school's student council, captain of the basketball team, and an honor roll student.[14] As a tutor, Myers was able to help acclimate the PREP students to what college life was really like. He tutored the students and lodged in the same dormitory as the visiting youngsters. He made extra efforts to get to know the Prepsters, often sharing his own stories as a way to connect with the younger students. Leet had assigned him to coordinate PREP's York and Harrisburg study centers. This meant that Myers had to be organized enough to manage his own studies while traveling to neighboring cities to tutor the high schoolers.

PREP carried a respectable and well-intentioned reputation for reaching out to both urban and economically disadvantaged high school students. Leon "Buddy" Glover, a Prepster who had graduated from McCaskey High School and who was admitted to Gettysburg College much because of his participation in the program, affirmed, "F&M was the clear leader on diversity."[15] Because of this, the number of African American students at Franklin and Marshall increased considerably. By the fall semester of 1967, forty-six full-time African American students were enrolled at the college. "In many ways," explained PREP tutor LeRoy Pernell, '71, "[Franklin and Marshall] was certainly trying to reach out to [African American] individuals." The college recruited Pernell, the first in his family to go to college, out of George Wingate High School located in Brooklyn's Bedford-Stuyvesant neighborhood because of his high SAT score. Although he was not well traveled—he was seventeen years old when he took his first trip beyond the boroughs of New York—Pernell chose to attend the predominantly white school in Pennsylvania's Dutch Country because he was, admittedly, "impressed that a school reached out the way that Franklin and Marshall did."[16]

By 1969, the number of African American students at Franklin and Marshall College reached fifty-eight. Yet as Franklin and Marshall's nonwhite enrollment increased, so did the divide among its students. There were still thirty white students to every African

American on campus. Lew Myers explained in a pamphlet to potential F&M recruits, "Everywhere you look—white! Profs, secretaries, staff members, lay employees, students, students, students … Most likely you'll have a white roommate your freshman year." He commented, however, "Things aren't as bad as they sound, simply because the white students don't bug you." It was clear that whites and blacks coexisted on campus without any problems. There appeared to be an "unwritten code" between the two races. "If you want to swing with white people, then you can jump into that bag," said Myers. "If you don't dig associating with white people you don't have to, other than attending class together." There was no campus policy that enforced segregation. Whether he believed it himself, Myers concluded, "It's really a beautiful situation."[17]

Yet still, Franklin and Marshall's black students needed to function around other black students. Since it was virtually an all-white campus, there were legitimate concerns of forgetting one's roots. Many black students were apprehensive about spending too much time with their white counterparts, unsure how it would be perceived. The lifestyle on campus was that one either was in a fraternity or seen as a social pariah. If one decided not to join a fraternity, then that student did not exist as a social being on campus. That was the snubbing reality for black students there. Eleven national fraternities operated at the college. Just two, Pi Lambda Phi and Zeta Beta Tau—both predominantly Jewish fraternities—openly welcomed black members.* The college's board of trustees maintained a policy of integration regarding fraternities, but most of the Greek houses on campus behaved in a way that was opposed to that policy. As a

---

* Today, Pi Lambda Phi and Zeta Beta Tau are both defunct at Franklin and Marshall College.

result, those in the black student community chose to be part of a marginalized nonentity on campus.[18]

Clearly, black and white students had different experiences when they walked on campus. Most of Franklin and Marshall's black students arrived from urban areas of the Northeast and South. The environment of Lancaster made it easy for those students to feel alienated, even regretful of the decision to attend the college. That alienation was magnified by the bizarre surroundings of Lancaster County. Alone and disoriented, most students found even the smell of cow manure too much to manage. LeRoy Pernell arrived from Brooklyn in 1967 and later remembered his first weekend at Franklin and Marshall. He said, "I looked out the window and I'm thinking, *Oh my God, where am I? Why am I here?* I'm seeing Amish. I had never seen that before. I didn't even know what it was."[19] African American students like Pernell were lost in the absence of typical social connections that make the college experience enjoyable. Of a total college enrollment of seventeen hundred students, the few African Americans bonded with each other naturally. There were outside influences that tied those bonds tighter, such as the Martin Luther King assassination and the Black Arise group that diffused its influence around town. Much that went into uniting black students was an effort to find social allies who had shared experiences and political viewpoints. Pernell said, "The black community in Lancaster was certainly part of that."

Indeed, Pernell, Myers, and their peers pursued a way to create a social life. "Now African American students may have been one of the first groups who did not find the fraternities attractive," Myers would recall in 2014.[20] Most avoided white fraternities because they failed to provide the social experiences that black students desired. "You get tired of those psychedelic bands and jerky dancing," Myers remarked.[21] Most of the black students at F&M received financial aid and thus did not have extra money for a social life, to fund special projects, to arrange transportation to and from other colleges, or to finance visiting speakers. Black students needed a frat house or organization that their social lives could evolve around. Most of all, they needed something to resemble their neighborhoods at home.[22]

To remedy the situation, African American students began voicing their grievances to Franklin and Marshall's administration. In May 1967, twelve black students met with the college's dean, the registrar, the financial aid officer, and trusted faculty to explain their desire to create a black student union. The administrative team was receptive. But since it was spring and final exams were near, the twelve students delayed plans for an official black student union until the fall. After the summer break, Franklin and Marshall's diminutive number of black students arrived to campus in August 1967 with a plan. Within the first week of the semester, an organizational meeting was held, where officers were elected, committees formed, and projects outlined. The black students now had their home away from home.

It was called the Afro-American Society. The Society, Lew Myers said proudly, "can be a crying towel, a pants kicker, a source of inspiration, or a source of information."

"The primary responsibility of the Society," Myers noted, "was to improve the social life for black students." The third-floor Rauch section of the Benjamin Franklin Residence Hall was designated for parties and card games. The students dubbed it Afro Hall. Myers recalls nostalgically, "It's the closest thing to 'the block' F&M has."[23] Responding to issues of social fraternities on campus and no female coeds, the Afro-American Society dedicated a sum of its money and some of its energy on busing in hundreds of black coeds from

Cheyney State College, Hood College, and Beaver College (present-day Arcadia University). On rare occasions, the Society reached out to female students at smaller liberal arts schools in Pennsylvania like Wilson, Dickinson, Gettysburg, and Swarthmore Colleges.

Membership requirements for the Afro-American Society were simple. All a student had to be was black. All members were male until the 1969–1970 school year, the first year that female students were accepted into Franklin and Marshall College. Membership was free, but dues were collected as the organization saw fit. The Society was an official college organization; because of this, the Dean's Office partially funded operations with no strings attached.

And yet as the founders contemplated the purpose of the Afro-American Society, they came to see it as a channel to promote their political agenda. It is true that nonwhite students at Franklin and Marshall were socially cold-shouldered. The original documents show this as the primary reason for forming the Society. Even more, however, there was a level of political consciousness that needed to be expressed. The question for black students was, "How do we who have this opportunity of education take that opportunity and make it work in some way that will have an influence on the social changes that are happening?" Society cofounder LeRoy Pernell offered an answer: "We had to have a vehicle where we could concentrate our concerns."[24] The Afro-American Society solidified a political voice for all of Franklin and Marshall's black students.

The Society's leaders were students who had already obtained considerable reputations on campus. Samuel Reginald Jordan Jr., '68, the father of the Afro-American Society, had an imposing presence. His classmates considered him perfectly confident in his manner, remarkable, and in possession of a far-ranging intellect. By way of Washington, DC, Jordan arrived on campus as a focused English major already bent on racial militancy. Owing to his academic pursuits, he quickly became a popular columnist for the college's semiweekly newspaper, the *College Reporter*. His friends considered him brilliant. One peer remembered, "He could recite long passages of Chaucer and Shakespeare in Old English and [Modern] English vogue." Jordan was a natural leader. "Clearly Sam was going places," recalled Afro-American Society cofounder Benjamin Bowser. In August 1967, at the Society's inaugural meeting, Jordan was voted the organization's first president. "He was in one sense a perfect first president," admitted Bowser. "I mean, if you start an organization and you gotta have somebody who is going to represent you well, and you want a natural leader," he said, "Sam was the man."[25]

As founder and first president of the Afro-American Society, Jordan stood out among his peers as a seasoned, even rigid, already politicized black power activist. While enrolled at Franklin and Marshall, he was an active member of the Student Nonviolent Coordinating Committee (SNCC) in Washington, DC, where Stokely Carmichael was involved. He often vanished from campus to return to his home city to participate in SNCC and Black Panther demonstrations, but he would be back at campus in time to attend class. Though often away, he always returned to Franklin and Marshall to voice his concerns about the welfare of his race. Many of his columns in the *College Reporter* were comprised of personal manifestoes about the race situation in the country. In an October 1967 editorial, Jordan wrote a theoretical obituary for Martin Luther King's method of tactical nonviolence. "In those Ghandi [*sic*] days of beautiful, almost religious[,] passivity, we caught the hearts of Americans everywhere," Jordan wrote, but retractors "responded immediately with praise and nightsticks, with their blessings and firebombs … they responded with anti-welfare legislation; gerrymandered school districts; Cicero,

Ill.; increased unemployment; Lester Maddox; and Boston's Mrs. Hicks."* He delivered a transparent message that rung in the mantra of Stokely Carmichael: "We resolved that no responsible black man could ask his brothers to march as sheep against an armed enemy." He also wrote a biting editorial criticizing Lancaster's hometown hero Barney Ewell, a track-and-field Olympian, for opposing the position taken by black athletes in 1968 to boycott the Olympic Games.[26]

Jordan's paradigm in the effort for racial justice roused action by classmates at Franklin and Marshall. Nonetheless, he had help in his popularity. On one special event weekend in 1968, Jordan and some friends obtained access to a campus car and attended a concert at Swarthmore College. There, Jordan met Fania E. Davis (whom he ended up dating and eventually marrying), the sister of Angela Davis, who at that time was just getting involved with the Black Panthers and the American Communist Party. As a newcomer in the Black Panther Party in Southern California, Angela Davis was participating

* Democratic governor of Georgia Lester Maddox campaigned in 1966 by using an axe handle as a symbol of resistance against integration. He reached prominence as owner of Pickrick Restaurant in 1964 when he refused to serve three African American students from Georgia Tech. His action was in blatant defiance of the newly passed Civil Rights Act.

Louise Day Hicks was a three-term Boston city councilwoman and one-term congresswoman. Hicks was nearly elected as mayor of Boston on a segregationist platform. As councilwoman and mayoral candidate, she refused to support the desegregation of Boston's public schools.

Cicero, Illinois, was a Chicago suburb known for its resistance to integration. On August 26, 1966, a march led by Martin Luther King and his Southern Christian Leadership Conference was announced. Before King and 250 marchers commenced their demonstration, 3,000 police officers and a large mob armed with bricks arrived to prevent the march.

in the development of a Liberation School in Los Angeles.* Jordan gathered ideas and inspiration from Angela's engagement in racial militancy through stories told to him by Fania.[27]

Fania was famous among the students at Franklin and Marshall, who were impressed by her air of confidence, exquisite beauty, and incomparable intellect. "She knew stuff that we didn't know," Lew Myers, a classmate of Jordan's, noted. "We were in Lancaster, and Fania went to school close to Philly. And with her sister's involvement, Fania was just so impressive."[28] Angela's rapidly growing popularity boosted Fania's reputation throughout Lancaster. The students knew Fania, partied with her, and were joined by her at several functions; however, not many of them can think back forty years to remember details about her level of engagement. "I paid very close attention to the Afro-American Society because I was one of the people who advocated for it, and I wanted to see it there [at F&M]," admitted Bowser, "so if Fania was ever at a meeting, I should remember that."[29] Though a legacy on campus, Fania's presence with Sam was genuinely known in Lancaster City. The couple had quite a foothold in the Seventh Ward, where they occasionally gathered at the Black Arise headquarters on Green Street. Sam, from the District of Columbia, and Fania, from Birmingham, were two of the new breed of activists

---

* It is worth noting that between 1967 and 1968, Angela Davis was a member of the Student Nonviolent Coordinating Committee at UCLA and a new member of the Che Lumumba Club, an all-black committee of the Communist Party–USA dedicated to the black liberation movement. During the summer of 1969, Davis embarked on a trip to Cuba to see what the socialist revolution had produced. Before her Cuba trip, Davis was hired by UCLA to teach philosophy. She was scheduled to begin teaching in the fall of 1969, but the board of regents fired her before she taught her first class. Davis's termination from the UCLA faculty propelled her onto the national stage. Fania Davis and Sam Jordan met each other before Angela Davis's trip to Cuba and her subsequent, and temporary, dismissal from the UCLA faculty. Davis fought the termination and won.

with allies in several cities moving in and out of furtive black power gatherings and communist meetings.[30]

The two were very influential in Lancaster City, but Sam seemed to be the more dynamic of the couple. "He seemed to be the force, not her," noted Afro-American Society member Jim Craighead.[31] Jordan's connection to Black Arise appeared in an edition of *Jet* magazine, published some time later. It testified as follows:

> [Samuel] Jordan was active in a Lancaster group called Black Arise, organizing blacks around issues such as high rent and, particularly, around an issue involving several black children who drowned in an open creek. After mass demonstrations and organizing, city fathers erected a fence around the creek.[32]

Jordan possessed the ability to organize remarkable events on campus that combined students and his associates from the city. His last act as president of the Afro-American Society was in March 1968 when he was instrumental in inviting Muhammad Ali to Franklin and Marshall's campus. Ali's visit was just the event to rattle the college's comfort level. Two years earlier, Ali had been at the crest of his career, but he'd had his boxing license suspended for his refusal to report to his physical examination after being called by the United States Selective Service. Ali spent his time away from boxing speaking about his conversion to Islam. There was nothing gentle about Ali's comments to the crowd that gathered at Hensel Hall to hear him. He spoke about racial separation and black empowerment. Since he represented Black Muslims, Ali reproached violence, claiming instead that "total separation of black people and white people" was the only solution for America's race problem. He cited the divided appearance of his audience, noting that black listeners were seated in the front and whites in the back. "That's one thing I like about this college," Ali jabbed. "You got the black folks in the front and the white folks in the back. That's real black power." He finished with an affirmation directed at Jordan and the Afro-American Society members: "You're taking over around here."[33]

Benjamin P. Bowser, '69, succeeded Jordan as the Society's president.* Bowser arrived on campus from New York City, where he had attended the prestigious Power Memorial Academy, an all-male Catholic prep school located in Midtown Manhattan. He was an honor student at Power Memorial, where classmate and future Basketball Hall of Famer Lew Alcindor (later known as Kareem Abdul-Jabbar) led the school to the 1964 high school basketball national championship. Bowser, a sociology major at Franklin and Marshall, was easy on the eyes, thin, and strong-minded. He was known for walking around campus with a pensive expression, sometimes wearing black-framed glasses, and stirring up debates. For two years he was a disc jockey for the campus radio station, WWFM. Bowser grew up following the progressive jazz movement in Harlem. As he looked for a form of entertainment in Lancaster, Pennsylvania, he found enjoyment playing emcee. And his show was popular. He noted, "I mainly played progressive jazz, and that was an extension of what I was doing in my [dorm] room."[34]

Feeling corralled by Lancaster County's dullness, Bowser found ways to occupy his time at Franklin and Marshall by getting involved off campus. By his junior year, Bowser was a driving force for off-campus student activities. He worked as a PREP tutor during his last two summers at the college. He was a Big Brother for the Student

---

* Bowser was elected as the Afro-American Society's second president in April 1968. He served in that capacity until April 1969, when Lewis Thrash was elected the Society's third president.

War on Poverty Program. Bowser volunteered as a Big Brother at the city school district's Higbee Elementary School tutoring adolescents in mathematics. "I was a mentor to a boy named Timothy Riggins," he reflected nostalgically. "I was the example, and he was the young person I was working with to improve his skills and get him thinking about college." His SWOP duties included visiting community recreation centers on evenings and weekends, visiting the elderly and shut-ins, volunteering time to the projects of Lancaster's Redevelopment Authority in the Seventh Ward, and giving speeches at McCaskey High School.[35]

The Afro-American Society had other leaders who complemented Jordan and Bowser. Lew Myers, '68, the aforementioned assistant director of special programs for the college's Pre-College Enrichment Program, was on the Afro-American Society's steering committee. Myers was a jack-of-all-trades student who attended the college on a work-study scholarship. He sang in the Chapel Choir and was a member of the Sociology Club. He played on the college's basketball team his freshman and sophomore years. During Myers's senior year, Franklin and Marshall president Keith Spalding convinced him to travel the Mid-Atlantic area recruiting African American high schoolers out of schools in Baltimore, Washington, DC, and New York. He made Dean's List his final three semesters at Franklin and Marshall, and was the Afro-American Society's first vice president. He found time to work alongside Benjamin Bowser on projects for the Student War on Poverty Program.

A keenly attentive Lewis R. Thrash, '71, became the third president of the Afro-American Society. Thrash, a serious advocate for black liberation, possessed a surfeit of wisdom. He was broad, neatly muscled, six feet tall, and handsome, with soft brown eyes and a deep voice. Considered a straight shooter by his close friends,

Thrash was seen by most people on campus as an overly determined individual. He enrolled at the Lancaster County liberal arts college from New Haven, Connecticut. On the basketball team his freshman year, he stopped playing after one season. He was a Thomas Gilmore Apple Prize recipient, the prize being a monetary award given to a sophomore for using his influence "for the best ideals of character and leadership."[36] Part of Thrash's notoriety on campus was due to his success as a sportswriter for the *College Reporter.*

One of his peers, a government major, the Afro-American Society secretary, and the star halfback on the football team, Harold Dunbar, called him Black Power Lew, particularly because Thrash also wrote incendiary columns in the campus newspaper endorsing black liberation. The moniker was catchy, so his classmates called him by that nickname until the time he graduated. In his columns, Thrash unleashed piercing attacks on the white power structure at the college. In pieces titled "Racial Harmony," "A Subterfuge," and "Waiting for Nixon," he laid out reasons why blacks and whites should live in separate societies. "Integration is only a subterfuge for the maintenance of white supremacy," he wrote. "White people had better start helping themselves, because it will be them, and not the black man, who will be responsible for the collapse of this country if it occurs."[37]

Thrash spoke for himself in his columns. Unfortunately, his editorials may have brought controversy to the Afro-American Society. Since Thrash was a sharp-penned columnist who was also a member of the Society, he spent a lot of time defending his organization's credibility. "One of the reasons the society was formed was to improve the black man's plight at F and M," he said. "I don't feel that the organization is racist. We don't have any particular policy about white America." The Society did not express racial separatism, but it did toe a fine line. "If we took a policy of black separatism some in the black community wouldn't agree with that," admitted Thrash. On the other hand, he continued, "if we advocated a policy of integration some of the community [might] call us 'Uncle Tom.'"[38] For Thrash there was no doubt that maintaining a strong image was high on his agenda.

The fourth president of the Afro-American Society was a fiery-tongued LeRoy Pernell. A member of the Class of 1971, Pernell, a government major, was a jazz lover from Brooklyn with an eye on becoming a teacher. After receiving mediocre grades during his freshman year, he faced the regrettable reality of having to drop out only to be drafted to serve in Vietnam. Pernell returned as a focused sophomore. He became the recipient of the college's Lanious B. Keiper Prize, a $1,000 endowment given to the most academically improved sophomore. Still proud of his turnaround, he joked many years later, "I went from one Dean's List to the other."[39] Pernell was a young man at five feet eleven inches with short dark hair and a goatee. He was sometimes seen wearing a dashiki and grasping a cane that had the appearance of an African staff.

Pernell was politically astute, very involved, and incredibly proud. A gruff, take-charge man, he found a unique way to embed himself in Lancaster's Seventh Ward. His trips to the city were attempts to develop cultural awareness among the area's teenagers. He directed one-act plays. "We would get some scripts and I would get some high school kids together," Pernell recalled with gratification.[40] His productions were performed at either Franklin and Marshall's Green Room Theater or at the one of the Seventh Ward community buildings. Pernell's involvement in the Seventh Ward afforded him many relationships, one of which was with NAACP president and social reform activist Rev. Ernest Christian, who officiated his wedding on May 15, 1971, just days before Pernell graduated from Franklin and Marshall.

In the black community of Lancaster, black power meant self-defense and racial autonomy; on Franklin and Marshall's campus, it meant going into town to invest in the community. The Seventh Ward longed for help. Jordan, Myers, Pernell, Bowser, Thrash, and other reputable, educated, and capable African American students dedicated themselves to that community's empowerment. Although they attended a predominantly white liberal arts college and were stuck behind ivy walls, they would not use that as an impediment to neglect the needs of the people in the Seventh Ward. Many years later, Myers explained the town–gown relationship: "We were blessed to be at F&M getting a good education. Just all the other stuff going on, the war, the death of Malcolm X, and more—we understood that there were folks out there needing help. None of us were as pure as the driven snow. That's why our class connected with the Seventh Ward more than the other classes [did]." Even though they were not from Lancaster, F&M's black students were adopted into it. "Many of us grew up [in similar communities] and clearly understood what it was like to live in the Seventh Ward," expounded an emphatic Lew Myers. "We could identify with those guys. We didn't turn our noses down to those guys, because we were them."[41] Accordingly, F&M's black collegians found ways to make constructive use of their time by spending free moments in the city's southeast.

The Afro-American Society prided itself on this form of social revitalization. As mentioned previously, it was called the town–gown relationship, where out-of-town college students got along with native townspeople. The black town–gown relationship in Lancaster was extraordinary. Students from campus and citizens from the southeast partied together. They did much more than that, however, as many of the social gatherings between Seventh Warders and Afro-American Society members turned into ugly spats of romantic contest. As college students visited the community more frequently, it became apparent that their motives were not always political.

At this moment in the sixties, Franklin and Marshall was still an all-male college. "We were going to see some girls, so we just went downtown—and that's where the girls were, in the Seventh Ward," Myers notes. "We went to parties, and guys [from the ward] would just get upset." The desire to meet black women became a noticeable incentive for making the three-mile journey from campus to the Seventh Ward. "Lots of black women of the Seventh Ward were very infatuated with these quality eligible men," explains Seventh Ward resident Buddy Glover, and "it led to some territorial turf battles."[42] Myers confirms Glover's assertion: "We were at F&M and that was a big deal. That created real friction."

Romantic rivalries aside, together with Black Arise, those from Franklin and Marshall were an inspiring support base for Stokely Carmichael's racial self-determination school of thought that permeated the race liberation movement, making activists feel obligated to serve, protect, and empower the black neighborhood. On campus, the Society held weekly meetings. Every other week, members held seminars that addressed relevant issues. Under its first president, Sam Jordan, the Afro-American Society met with Black Arise leaders at the Green Street headquarters every other month. The desire to work closely with Black Arise was written clearly on the front page of the Afro-American Society's decree. "The Black psyche has to broaden in a variety of ways," Benjamin Bowser, the declaration's author, declared. "The institution of a *Black school of thought* in conjunction with the Black Arise organization in Lancaster's black community is one of those ways."[43]

Naturally, the frequency of time spent in the Seventh Ward left the Franklin and Marshall students hopeful about generating financial interests in that part of the city. Their budget, like that of most student organizations, lacked appropriate funds. Bowser, accordingly, asked the college's administration to reach out to the Seventh Ward. "We would like the college to publicly support our efforts," he said, "by ... aiding in the establishment of a storefront in the Southeast Area." He believed that the college should also make an effort to employ "more black people in technical and clerical" positions on campus.[44]

Just because the Afro-American Society spent so much time in the city does not mean that its members neglected their academics on campus. The Society took great strides to go beyond its purely social function. It attempted to devise an academic plan for its members, helping students get totally immersed in their work. For one, veteran leaders saw incoming freshmen as being vulnerable to exploitation. "We knew who the snakes were in the faculty. We knew who to avoid, so it naturally evolved into a support organization," explained Bowser.[45] In fact, the study methods that the Society employed were unparalleled. It maintained a four-hour tutor program Monday and Thursday evenings at the library for "each brother" who had academic difficulties. They called these tutor groups "study cells." Study cells concentrated most on helping freshmen exercise study skills during their first year at Franklin and Marshall. The Society's Academic Committee claimed, "We make sure you don't fall asleep at the books or get up every 15 minutes to wander around." It challenged, "See how much work you can get done."[46]

Clearly, academic success was vital for the Society's credibility. Before the Afro-American Society was formed in 1967, the dropout rate of black students at Franklin and Marshall was approximately 40 percent. The mean grade point average of the college's nonwhite students—all four classes combined—was 2.0. Society cofounder Lew Myers acknowledged that most African American students were not prepared for the rigor of college life. "It was just that level of [academics] that we had to get used to," recalled Myers years later. "Some guys just never really could get into that kind of grind."[47] After one year, the Society credited itself with decreasing the dropout rate to 3 percent. Benjamin Bowser and Lew Thrash gloated in a fund-raising letter, "Only one brother did not return for '68–'69."[48]

Most critically, the Afro-American Society aimed to establish a Department of Black Studies with a variety of courses that would examine all facets of African American political, economic, and cultural life. It wanted the college to hire black counselors who could help African American students adjust to life on a virtually all-white campus, and recruit black professors who could help African Americans find an identity in the community where they lived. The Society suggested that administration officials should find a way to either hire "visiting black professors" or to "finance" student visits to "black scholars at other schools."

Moreover, those in the Society demanded a house off campus for Franklin and Marshall's black students. All of Franklin and Marshall's black students lived in dormitories on campus, whereas many white students occupied Greek houses off campus. Benjamin Bowser implied that an off-campus house for the Afro-American Society could "expand our activities and serve as the nucleus for black thought and black life." One of Bowser's signature accomplishments was his having convinced the college's administration to allow the Society to occupy an empty building called the Annex and use it as a Black Culture Center. It was a way to link the college's African American students' social lives with their civic enterprises. The center's intentions were multifaceted. First, it was to become home for the Afro-American Society. There, the members could discuss issues of the day, debate viewpoints, devise methods for self-improvement, or simply turn on the television to watch a game and relax. The space also welcomed black teenagers from the city to get involved in their various programs. Bowser intended that the cultural center include a museum, a library, study rooms, a seminar room, and a coffee shop to feed students who grew hungry after midnight.[49] He wanted a place where the white community could learn more about the history and status of blacks in America. Finally, Bowser envisioned that the Black Culture Center would become a "complement" to the proposed black studies department.

There is something remarkable about the speed with which the Afro-American Society became an important part of Franklin and Marshall campus life. More than anything else, the Society's instant influence on campus, in the city, and on black students at other colleges seems to testify to the deep-seated need for leadership during a complicated period.

Under the presidency of Bowser, the Society began publishing an intercollegiate scholastic magazine called the *Black Collegiate*. It helped propagate the Black Panthers' "black school of thought" by combining two goals of the Society's philosophy: serving as a forum to circulate political doctrine and as an avenue of expression for students with creative urges.[50] *Black Collegiate* cofounder Jim Craighead described the magazine as a medium to distribute the thoughts of Franklin and Marshall's black students to those at other colleges. He said the *Black Collegiate* "promoted and gave guidance for what we should be doing as black students for the communities that we were involved in: our school community, our communities at home, and the United States of America."[51] The *Black Collegiate* helped the Afro-American Society become the model organization for colleges in central and southeastern Pennsylvania. Black students at Wilson, Dickinson, Gettysburg, Albright, Millersville State, Beaver, and Penn State–Capitol City all examined the Society's services in forming similar organizations.[52]

Society funds were limited, however, so the magazine was published "on an issue-by-issue basis" over the course of three years, 1968 to 1970, rather than weekly, monthly, or quarterly. The *Black Collegiate* became the Society's best literary attempt to extend Franklin and Marshall's black culture to African American students at other colleges and universities. "The views presented are not to be taken as absolute or padded," elucidated Bowser, so as to not turn away readers. He warned, "The students were allowed to write whatever they perceived[,] and their texts have been published in [their] entirety."[53] Each publication was marketed for distribution to schools in the tristate area: New York, New Jersey, and Pennsylvania.

The *Black Collegiate* was a sweet source of black aesthetics. Likewise, it existed as a precursor for curriculum that could make up the much-desired black studies program. Each edition included publications of art, poetry, cartoons, and short stories produced by black Franklin and Marshall students. Lew Thrash described the magazine as "an attempt to contribute to the building of a black culture." Bowser was the publication's first editor in 1968. Thrash and LeRoy Pernell served in that role in 1969 and 1970 respectively.

There was one more item on the Society's agenda, one that would cause much friction on campus. As early as 1967, students demanded a minor or major field offered in black studies. For this, the school was not so willing to conform.

Meanwhile, 115 miles south of Franklin and Marshall, about twelve hundred of the eighty-two hundred students at Howard University occupied an administration building on campus. For five days beginning on March 20, the protesters lay in to demand the reinstatement of thirty-nine students who were expelled for disrupting the college's annual Charter Day ceremonies by taking over the podium and making a multitude of demands, including the formation of a student judiciary, establishment of a Black Awareness Institute, and a change in curriculum that was, according to Gary Ayres, president of the Association of Men Students at Howard, "relevant to the black community."[54] The disturbance at the historically black university located just north of 1600 Pennsylvania Avenue was the nation's first black student takeover. Many such takeovers on campuses across the United States were to follow, including Columbia University's violent takeover a few weeks later. However, it must be noted that the demands put forth by students at Howard concentrated on issues greater than black power. Their demands centered on black consciousness. They hungered for knowledge about African history and African American culture. "We think this university should prepare us to be leaders in the black community," said normally soft-spoken and mild-mannered Joseph Middlebrooks, president of the Engineering and Architectural Students Association. "Instead, what it's doing is preparing us to fit into the white man's world—and not in leadership roles." Howard students believed the university should be a center of talent and knowledge for national efforts to attack the problems of poverty and discrimination. While the takeover at Howard was frightening and unpredictable, it served as an ideal vessel of motivation for hundreds of black collegians across the United States who believed in Stokely Carmichael's reform ideology of black nationalism.[55]

Chapter 5

THE CRISIS

THE DEPTH OF discontent among those involved in the black power movement, whether in academia or on the streets, was intensified on the evening of April 4, 1968, when, just after six o'clock, Martin Luther King Jr. was shot while standing on the balcony of the Lorraine Motel in Memphis, Tennessee. He was pronounced dead an hour later at St. Joseph's Hospital.

The assassination created a surge of violence that swept across the United States. Black power leader Stokely Carmichael urged African Americans to arm themselves and "kill off the real enemy." At a press conference held at Howard University, Carmichael proclaimed, "We have to retaliate for the death of our leaders. The execution of those deaths will not be in the courtrooms. They will be in the streets."[1] This call reverberated through nearly every black community in the country. Just hours after the announcement of King's death, angry crowds in Lancaster, according to the *Lancaster New Era*, "broke windows, looted stores, threw firebombs that started many blazes and attacked police with guns, stones and bottles."[2] Other violent reactions occurred in the District of Columbia, Oakland, Houston, Detroit, Chicago, and Pittsburgh.

The headline in the *Lancaster New Era* read, "City Curbs Crowds After Stoning and Looting in S.E. Area." Five stores in the Seventh Ward were looted the night of King's death. The Sanitary Food Market at 466 S. Duke Street was ransacked for $2,000 worth of food and $600 in cigarettes. Harry J. Yoffee, the Jewish storeowner, had his car windshield smashed. At 9:35 p.m., windows of Blum's Outlet Store at 504 S. Duke Street were broken. While the break-in at Blum's Outlet Store was taking place, a motorist driving along Woodward Street had a brick thrown through his windshield. Two stores on the same block, Wenger's Grocery Store and Siegel Grocery Store, were robbed. At 11:10 p.m. a garbage can was used to break through the front window at Herson's Grocery Store at 702 S. Duke Street. Before midnight, three more shops were looted. Weis Cleaners at 320 S. Lime St., Sam's Store at 201 Church St., and Washington House on the corner of Lime and Locust Streets were all victims of robberies.[3] Twelve vandalism cases and other reports of broken store and car windows occurred in Lancaster during the first twelve hours after King's death.

Black Arise leader Benjamin Bethea owns up to the fact that several residents from the Seventh Ward intended to plunder everything that fell before them, including a church. "There was a white church smack in the middle of the Seventh Ward, and we always said that we were going to burn it down." He confessed, "That night we burned it down." It was the Faith United Church of Christ, located on the corner of South Duke and North Streets. Many resented Faith UCC's presence in the area.[4] It had been erected in the middle of the Seventh Ward in the sixties when area redevelopment decimated many minority-owned businesses and relocated minority families.

The church's Gothic structure reminded residents of that subjugation. So Bethea and his friends set it on fire that evening.*

The scene in Lancaster was just as solemn the day after King was killed. On the morning of April 5, fifty visibly shaken black students walked out of McCaskey High School in an expression of sorrow. McCaskey principal John Rodman gave permission to Darryl Glover, a senior, and a committee of students to conduct what Glover called "liberation." Glover and his peers were upset that school was in session the day after King's tragic death. "What we're doing," Dr. C. M. Hill, assistant superintendent of Lancaster City Schools, explained to reporters, "is saying that if the children are so emotionally upset that they cannot cope in the classroom they can go home." Hill added in support, "We too, grieve for the man."[5]

Glover's "liberation" group made its way from the northern end of the city to the predominantly black Edward Hand Junior High School in the southeast. Chanting excessively outside the school, the throng demanded that their younger peers inside the school be excused from the building. Even Edward Hand, the only middle school located within Lancaster's southeast on South Anne Street, was vandalized amid the disturbances that occurred in the Seventh Ward hours after King's death. Glover and the marchers shouted for the students to come out of the building. One student remembered hearing shouts of, "Leave the oppressors!" and "Black power!" The faculty at Edward Hand was frightened. "The teachers didn't know what to do," recalled

---

* The construction of the new Higbee Elementary School, present-day MLK Elementary, was part of city redevelopment, leading to the destruction of the original Seventh Ward from Church Street to Chesapeake Street heading west to east. Businesses and homes were torn down and replaced with churches, the aforementioned school, and public housing. Seventh Ward residents went from homeowners to renters. Leon "Buddy" Glover, once a resident at 431 Green Street, recalled the experience as "painful and not necessary." Glover believes "the area never really recovered."

Gerald Wilson, at the time a ninth grader at Hand who was liberated during the demonstration. Information about the violence in the District of Columbia and other locations was no secret to those in Lancaster. "They had their radios on in their classrooms and heard about the riots and fires all over the country," explained Wilson. Adding to the hysteria were the police cruisers that circled the school that morning. "Next thing you know," he said, "teachers were in their cars and left. They got the hell out of there."[6]

After about twenty students from Edward Hand joined Glover's marchers, the demonstration proceeded to Penn Square, the city's center. At that moment there were approximately seventy participants, all under nineteen years old. "We have no plans at this time," Glover told a reporter, "other than to walk uptown to show our grief and how upset we really are."[7]

One of the student marchers was Seventh Ward resident Doug Dennison, local football hero and future running back for the Dallas Cowboys. Dennison made comments that indicated his empathy for Black Arise, headquartered a short distance from his house. He said, "[King] was trying to do everything the right way; now this gives Black Power a chance to step in." He then added a prescient comment: "There should be a national shrine [for Dr. King], which Negroes could look up to, for him—he was a great leader."[8]

After convening at Penn Square, Lancaster City mayor Thomas Monaghan spoke to the group, expressing that he "understood their feelings." The mayor suggested that they attend the memorial service at Franklin and Marshall College that afternoon.

The remembrance at Franklin and Marshall College was the largest public demonstration for Martin Luther King in Lancaster, but nothing went smoothly. The event, held inside a softly lit Hensel Hall, featured speeches from the college's faculty. The Franklin and Marshall officials hoped the event would help heal the local community. Instead, many in the audience were sour, even resentful, especially the black college students. "I remember leaving early," said Benjamin Bowser, vice president of the college's Afro-American Society. "In fact, I may have even walked out." Many did the same. "We knew of the people on the faculty and administration and among students who really did not embrace King's legacy," he said. "Then to have these people come up the very next day and give even ritualistic praise of King was a bit much."[9] Likewise, many in Glover's McCaskey contingent followed Bowser and the Franklin and Marshall students out the door.

There was something that troubled the black student body that day. On their minds were the disturbances that followed King's death. The turmoil affected more than just Lancaster's Seventh Ward community; the disturbances were widespread. Both sets of students felt that the memorial service had ignored those concerns. Some students had family and friends living in urban areas where some of the worst outbreaks of violence had occurred. Bowser lamented, "We didn't know if people were all right or if our homes were burning up."[10] Mourning over the loss of Martin Luther King was eclipsed by concern for family and friends. Those who spoke at the memorial service did not acknowledge those anxieties, Bowser implied. Nor did they consider that the students belonged to those communities. "That pissed us off," said Bowser.

Before they walked out, members of Franklin and Marshall's Afro-American Society were permitted to give remarks. Society member Emanuel Towns, '69, stated that he felt King's nonviolent methods generated only violence, hatred, and more indifference. Towns said, "No longer can I look at the white race as a whole without contempt ... We will mobilize our forces to defeat you ... This war will without a doubt be violent and will be led against you by Blacks." Towns's remarks drew a standing ovation from black people in the audience. Once he finished, a member of the Afro-American Society presented a written testimonial to the media on his way out. While unrealistic, it passionately declared, "There remain only a few hours for you to do a life's work if you should desire to have a nation called the United States. For after those few hours the ends of the earth shall come together around your throats and you shall be totally destroyed. No longer do we say to ourselves, 'If there were only another way.' For we are now certain there is no other way."[11] The statement put everyone on alarm, especially that night as more looting and violence consumed the city.

An anxiety developed among officials that night as rumors circulated that people in the Seventh Ward were mobilizing. Prior to the King assassination, an unfinished construction project left a deep ditch up and down South Duke Street. On the evening of April 5, demonstrators with piles of rocks burrowed themselves into those trenches, ready to hurl their improvised mortars into the windshields of unfamiliar cars. The *Lancaster New Era* reported, "The most serious incident Friday night was the narrow escape of a Lancaster City police officer when a lone sniper's bullet ripped through his coat and struck his gun holster while he was on foot patrol." That officer was Frederick C. Wagaman Jr., who was shot at 10:00 p.m. while patrolling on the corner of Vine and S. Duke Streets. Just minutes later police took into custody an "unidentified man who was walking in the 100 block of S. Duke Street, carrying a .22 caliber rifle equipped with a telescopic sight." The suspect, described the *Lancaster New Era*, was released from custody the next morning, "having been absolved of any connection in the incident."[12]

The Lancaster Police Department blamed the violence on groups of "agitators" who arrived from the "outside." The outside agitators, the police department affirmed, gathered in crowds of between twenty-five and one hundred people in several locations aiming to incite "unrest in the city." Mayor Monaghan issued a statement saying that "'unfamiliar faces' had been noticed in the southeast area" of Lancaster.[13]

Statements like these certainly helped sway the locals to opine that many of the problems in Lancaster were caused by outsiders. That was the classic line of reasoning chosen by authorities seeking to offload blame to strangers of the community. Four decades later, in 2007, Bethea conceded that members of Black Arise, not "unfamiliar faces" to the city, had created the disorder. Bethea explained, "That night [police] tried to put foot patrol out and we would make them strip naked down to boxer shorts and go back to the police station." Bluntly, he said, "We busted out cop car windows [too]." The *Lancaster New Era* confirmed his statement. "At the end of the night," the report revealed, "a police check showed that car windows of two police cruisers had been smashed by thrown rocks."[14] There were, in fact, a few outsiders involved in the Seventh Ward chaos. Newspaper testimonies indicate a very small number of Franklin and Marshall College students present in the ward on April 4 and April 5. The leadership, nonetheless, emanated from folks in the city.[15]

It clearly appeared to Bethea that city cops were given the order to allow the Seventh Ward residents to let off steam. According to Bethea, "The police sat on the other side of Duke Street," while the looters stayed within the boundaries of the city's black neighborhood. They "let us vent," Bethea said. "We busted into supermarket stores and took all the food, and everywhere we went we took everything out and gave it, and distributed it, to the welfare recipients." He described it as "a Robin Hood thing." He did acknowledge that he and other Black Arise members were fortunate to escape arrest and subsequent prison sentences for their behavior. The police "didn't have the sophistication, no camcorders or anything," he said. "So we got away with a lot of things that night."[16]

Lancaster City Police Officer J. Donald Schaeffer has a different perspective: "We couldn't back off or [else] we'd have given them a free hand at everything they wanted to do." The conflicting opinions aside, things changed drastically after that night. City cops no longer patrolled the Seventh Ward on foot. "You couldn't do it on foot patrol anymore," explained Officer Schaeffer. "It was all two-man cars after that [night]."[17]

Leon "Buddy" Glover, a Seventh Warder who grew up next door to the Black Arise headquarters on Green Street, recalled in great detail the evenings following the King assassination. Glover was a Gettysburg College freshman who hitchhiked home the day after King died. On the evening of April 5, Glover was with the multitude who had gathered in the streets. "The police and mayor were not fully accurate" in their assessment, insisted Glover. "These were nights when those in Black Arise, maybe some outsiders, but [mostly] homegrowns [*sic*], took to the street in frustration." For its honesty, Glover's account may well prove him to be the paramount piece of evidence, a vital link in the chain of events explaining how many young men of the Seventh Ward community became radicalized for good. "The ward had become an occupied area with mostly white police and guardsmen with heavy military equipment," explained Glover. "It no longer felt like home that night, and violence was made acceptable as a reaction."[18]

On April 6, Mayor Monaghan levied a special set of rules upon the city. The curfew for juveniles was set for 7:00 a.m. to 7:00 p.m. Those who were twenty-one years or older had a curfew of 11:00 p.m.

No groups of more than five people were allowed on the street. Bars were closed at sundown. Restaurants could remain open after 9:00 p.m., but they were prohibited from selling alcohol.[19] Lancaster was never placed under martial law, but first-term governor Raymond Shafer called up a Lancaster-based National Guard unit to serve a "precautionary" role in subduing the violence. Officer Schaeffer remembers that the National Guard was there on standby for the city police. He said, "The National Guard didn't go in on anything until they were called in by the police department." Colonel David E. Reiber was the commanding officer of the 103rd Medical Battalion in Lancaster, with two of four companies based at Stahr Armory in the city. In addition to the 103rd Medical Battalion, other units dispatched to Lancaster were the 213th Maintenance Battalion and an aviation company of the 104th Armored Cavalry.[20]

It was not pretty, but by Sunday, April 7, the city commenced a crawl to normalcy. Vandalism had tapered off. People started to focus their attention on healing one another. That afternoon, the newspaper reported that nearly four hundred people, including a good mix between whites and blacks, gathered on the steps of the Lancaster County Courthouse to pay homage to the slain civil rights leader. Several civic and religious leaders eulogized King. It was clear to those in attendance, however, that the residue of racial anguish was spilling over the somber demonstration. Rev. Ernest Christian, the president of Lancaster's chapter of the NAACP, having replaced Kenneth Bost a year earlier, directed his comments to the white people in the crowd. "You have shot Martin Luther King. There will be another Martin Luther King. And you may shoot him, but there will be 13 million more Martin Luther Kings coming."

There was much tension in Christian's lead sentence. Angry, he intended to bring out the fury in a lot of people. The charge against all white people made the unsettled nature of race relations apparent. Christian was an outspoken minister who had a lot of influence among Lancaster's black youth. Born in Maryland in 1909, Christian arrived in Lancaster in 1928. After World War II, he took up a residence at 434 S. Christian Street in the heart of the Seventh Ward, and soon became a leader in the local branch of the NAACP.[21] By 1967, Rev. Christian became the president of the branch. A year before King's assassination, Christian had purchased a warehouse on the 400 block of Locust Street, located just around the corner from his house, and turned it into a youth center. Most adults and other clergy in the city were unsure about Christian, but teenagers seemed to flock to him. "He was more militant than others," said Seventh Ward resident Louis Butcher, who later became the pastor of Brightside Baptist Church, located a few miles from Christian's childhood home. Butcher explained the strong connection between Ernest Christian and the community's youth: "He challenged the system and had the ear of the young people because of that."[22]

Using the Lancaster County Courthouse as his backdrop, Christian urged the city's black youth to take action immediately. At least fifty African American men and women stood on the courthouse steps behind him as he warned, "If we don't have complete freedom, then I say whatever we do, you'll be responsible for it." Many held up signs that read, "Martin Luther King, you have not died in vain"; "Martin Luther King, the Apostle of Peace, is Dead"; "He who has lost his freedom has nothing else to lose. We have not lost"; and "We want yesterday's freedom now."[23]

Race relations in Lancaster took a very long time to reach civility. Not that the leaders in the community were incompetent. Events on the national stage seemingly sent racial affairs back into a state of sensitivity. Two months after King was murdered, presidential candidate Robert F. Kennedy was shot in California very early in the morning on June 5, 1968. A day later he died, leaving the nation without a prominent civil rights leader. Then, on October 16, Tommie Smith and John Carlos took the gold and bronze medals respectively in the 200-meter sprint at the Mexico City Summer Olympic Games. The nation was stunned to see the two shoeless men standing on the podium with their heads bowed and their fists raised in the black power salute during the national anthem.

In this charged atmosphere, the scene in Lancaster remained hostile for many months. It seems paradoxical to see black city residents attack stores and vehicles in their own neighborhood. The turmoil benefited Black Arise. Bethea said, "I saw a flip on a lot of people's philosophy" after the King assassination. "Because the life of a man of peace was taken that night [April 4]," he lamented, "a lot of people gave up on nonviolence." The death of King compelled angry and vulnerable people to turn violent. "If they are going to kill a man of peace, then there's no sense for us trying to be peaceful," Bethea rationalized. "So that's when we [i.e., Black Arise] got a lot of new recruits."

Gerald Wilson, a witness to the turmoil, validated Bethea's perspective. "Before that time," an inveterate Wilson said, "black people … basically stayed in their place." He continued, "When MLK got killed, that changed the whole perspective." The big comment from the community was, "Why are they destroying their own stuff?" Wilson explained, "Basically black people looked at it like this: 'This isn't our own, this isn't ours; we're just here in this place and time. We don't own any of this. This is just a greater society.' And they were striking back."[24]

This was the most explosive period in Lancaster during the twentieth century. The tragic fallout was yet to come.

Bird's-eye view of Franklin and Marshall College, 1910. Courtesy of 1953 *Oriflamme*, Franklin and Marshall College.

Sumner Bohee, '50, Franklin and Marshall College's first African American graduate. Courtesy of Oriflamme, Franklin and Marshall College.

Lewis Myers in 1968. Courtesy of *Oriflamme,*
Franklin and Marshall College.

LeRoy Pernell in 1971. COURTESY OF ORIFLAMME, FRANKLIN AND MARSHALL COLLEGE.

Samuel R. Jordan in 1968. Courtesy of *Oriflamme*, Franklin and Marshall College.

Benjamin Bowser in 1969. COURTESY OF *ORIFLAMME*, FRANKLIN AND
MARSHALL COLLEGE.

Hubert Martin in 1968. Courtesy of *Oriflamme*,
Franklin and Marshall College.

Robert Rivers in 1968. COURTESY OF *ORIFLAMME*,
FRANKLIN AND MARSHALL COLLEGE.

Harold Dunbar in 1969. Courtesy of *Oriflamme*,
Franklin and Marshall College.

Adebisi Otudeko in 1970. COURTESY OF ORIFLAMME, FRANKLIN AND
MARSHALL COLLEGE.

Donald Tyrrell in 1974. COURTESY OF *ORIFLAMME*,
FRANKLIN AND MARSHALL COLLEGE.

Leon Galis in 1970. Courtesy of *Oriflamme*, Franklin and Marshall College.

Gerald Enscoe in 1970. Courtesy of *Oriflamme*, Franklin and Marshall College.

Franklin and Marshall president Keith Spalding in 1967. COURTESY OF
ORIFLAMME, FRANKLIN AND MARSHALL COLLEGE.

Lou Athey in 1970. COURTESY OF *ORIFLAMME*, FRANKLIN AND MARSHALL COLLEGE.

Sidney Wise in 1967. COURTESY OF *ORIFLAMME*, FRANKLIN AND MARSHALL COLLEGE.

Mathematics professor Donald Western was given charge of the May 22, 1969, uprising investigation. COURTESY OF THE 1967 EDITION OF *ORIFLAMME*, FRANKLIN AND MARSHALL COLLEGE.

Goethean Hall, location of the hostage taking during the May 22, 1969, uprising. COURTESY OF *ORIFLAMME*, FRANKLIN AND MARSHALL COLLEGE.

This image shows African American students entering Goethean Hall at the start of the uprising. COURTESY OF DR. BENJAMIN P. BOWSER.

Lewis Thrash with his twin sons, Alimayu (left) and Jameel, in 1977. COURTESY OF ALIMAYU THRASH.

Chapter 6
THE EXPLOSION

S AM JORDAN EMERGED as Franklin and Marshall's most radical activist. From one vantage point, it might be considered unfortunate that Jordan's intellect was outweighed by his fanaticism in the black power cause. His extremism got him into serious legal trouble weeks after the Martin Luther King assassination and just days before his own graduation from Franklin and Marshall College.

On May 10, 1968, Jordan was arrested for taking part in Black Arise's bombing of the Selective Service office at 50 S. Duke Street in the Seventh Ward (as mentioned previously, in chapter 3). Jordan, a twenty-one-year-old senior when this incident occurred, was arrested at gunpoint on the corner of Lime Street and Howard Avenue just before 3:00 a.m. carrying a Molotov cocktail in one hand and a .38-caliber pistol in the other. The arresting officer, David Dommel, reported that the gun was loaded with six rounds. Lancaster City police later discovered five jugs of "highly-corrosive acid" hidden "in a laundry bag on a chair in the middle of his dorm room" at 301 Dietz Hall. They suggested that it was going to be used to make explosives. Along with the chemicals, Police Detective Luther Henry claimed to have confiscated a clock mechanism that could be used for a timing device for a bomb. Jordan was charged with carrying explosives, carrying a concealed deadly weapon, violating the Uniform Firearms Act, and possessing explosives.[1] Jordan's bail was set at $32,000.

In retrospect, this action is comprehensible considering how tumultuous the spring of 1968 was in the United States. Only weeks before Jordan's arrest, Martin Luther King was tragically killed and General William Westmoreland requested that another two hundred thousand soldiers be sent to Vietnam. Such moments were provocations for radicalness. But still, there were those in Lancaster who believed Jordan had been set up. Seventh Ward resident Louis Butcher, who graduated from Franklin and Marshall College in 1965 and was presently working for the Lancaster County Human Relations Commission, testified at Jordan's trial that Jordan was in the ward that night "helping to keep people calm." Butcher remarked, with his power and influence, that Jordan was often the voice of reason when ruffians looked to be on the verge of doing damage.[2] Another Seventh Warder, Gerald Wilson, remembered hearing rumors about Jordan's arrest: "There is no way he'd be stupid enough to walk around with a firebomb," said Wilson, who later became a city police officer. "He [always] said the cops set him up, maybe even put the bomb in his pocket."[3]

Yet several newspaper accounts unmistakably reported that there were at least fifteen people from the Seventh Ward who were involved in firebombing the Lancaster draft offices ten minutes after Jordan was arrested. There were other reports of young people rummaging around the Seventh Ward with homemade explosives. The *Intelligencer Journal* reported, "Pop and wine bottles filled with gasoline and oil and armed with rag wicks" were discovered in the neighborhood. Detectives recovered ten abandoned firebombs in backyards and alleys of the ward. Overall, almost $1,000 of damages was done to the draft offices.[4]

The students at Franklin and Marshall were in shock. Even those closest to Jordan were stunned to hear about his arrest. "There were two Sam Jordans," noted Benjamin Bowser, who later became a professor of sociology at California State University, East Bay. "There was the Sam Jordan at college and the Sam Jordan would-be SNCC activist." Jordan had earned a reputation of disappearing for days at a time, leaving his friends at college in the dark about his whereabouts. Bowser recalled, "[Jordan] seemed to know people in the black student movement in the South," where he spent a lot of time working voter registration. "He was very private. None of us on campus knew much about him," admitted Bowser.

The arrest made for a strenuous twenty-four hours on campus. The police thought Jordan had accomplices with him from Franklin and Marshall in addition to Black Arise members from the city. Jordan's arrest made each African American and some members of Students for a Democratic Society at Franklin and Marshall suspects in the bombings. "If any of us were out that night, we clearly would have been arrested," said Bowser. "If we had been coming from in town, or coming from out of town, or for that matter had short-cutted [*sic*] from one location to another on campus, we could have been caught up in something that we didn't know was going on."[5]

As Jordan sat in the Lancaster County Prison, his friends on campus reached out to Black Arise's Black People's Defense League. "Brother Samuel Jordan faces a similar fate at the hands of the racists Lancaster County Police force," declared two of Jordan's Franklin and Marshall peers, Hubert Martin and Robert Rivers, who were volunteering as secretaries for the Defense League. "We cannot let his arrest go unchallenged. We cannot allow nothing to be done concerning the outrageous bail set for his release."[6] From the sum of money gathered, the Defense League helped hire civil rights attorneys Harry Lore of Philadelphia and Menno B. Rohrer of Lancaster to serve as Jordan's lawyers.

After hearing the plea from Lore and Rohrer, Judge William G. Johnstone reduced the bail to $17,000. Jordan's father arrived three days later from the District of Columbia to pay the bail. Jordan graduated from Franklin and Marshall College a month later.[7]

Jordan, who during the intervening time was accepted into the graduate school at New York State University to undertake psychology and social work, returned to Lancaster in September to stand trial. He testified to Judge W. Hensel Brown that he was in the city to reason with several Black Arise members who were plotting to bomb the Selective Service offices. After receiving a voice message from classmate Robert Rivers at 2:15 a.m. telling him that trouble was developing in the city, he said, "I got dressed and walked down [to] the community."[8] He added, "I had been on several occasions a sort of meditator" for unrests in the Seventh Ward, including, as one witness testified, "play[ing] a leading part in discouraging 400 young people from wrecking the center of the city the night after Dr. Martin Luther King Jr. was assassinated." Jordan told the court, "I went [there] because I felt I could handle it." He explained to the judge that he had a revolver with him because it "might be more persuasive if I had a gun with me. It might be able to stop this." The community was already in upheaval well before his arrest. Over a hundred people were on the streets, and shots could be heard coming from the intersection of Rockland Street and Howard Avenue. Jordan stated that after he heard the gunfire, he "proceeded in that direction," upon reaching which he discovered a "half gallon jar, filled about one-third of the way with what smelled like gasoline" on Howard Avenue.

"I recognized this jar as a Molotov cocktail," he said, "and not being certain of the nature of the disturbance, I proceeded immediately to dispose of the bottle" at the nearest sewer inlet, which he believed would be at the corner of Howard Avenue and Lime Street. "I literally walked into a police officer with a rifle."[9] Two witnesses, Mr. and Mrs. Clifford D. Ham, a married couple who lived at 153 Howard Avenue, claimed that Jordan's pace was casual instead of his hurrying along with a keen hustle like he was determined to use the device. They both watched the arresting officer point a gun at Jordan and say, "One crooked move and you're dead."

The Jordan trial concluded on September 23, 1968, 136 days after his arrest. The jury found him guilty of all four charges.[10] After a round of appeals, the conviction was upheld in April 1969. Jordan was sentenced to the Eastern State Correctional Institute in Philadelphia for a term of one to two years. In addition, he had to pay court costs and fines, and spend several years on probation.[11] (He was released on parole on February 8, 1972.)

Afterward, Franklin and Marshall's Afro-American Society carried on with several of its off-campus programs without the leadership of their friend. The Society continued its outreach with Seventh Ward high schoolers who had recently formed a black student union at J. P. McCaskey High School, the only urban high school in Lancaster County.

Of the 2,100 students enrolled at McCaskey High School at the start of the 1968–1969 school year, about 180 were African American. The last week of October was considered Black History Week at the school. As a capstone to the week's events, the Black Student Union scheduled an assembly for Thursday, October 31. Accordingly, posters were displayed throughout the school's corridors, and periodic announcements produced some excitement about the event. Nancy

Val, a white sophomore, remembers, "At times there would be graffiti on their posters in the hallway. There were smart remarks and just little things here and there." Many had their doubts about the school's show. "Things were a little shaky," said Val about the days leading up to the assembly. "It was like sitting on eggshells, and I'm sure the administration was feeling that." Despite the jumpiness, the assembly commenced at 10:00 a.m. on October 31. "I can remember where I was sitting in the upper right section in the auditorium," said Val. "They had [on] beautiful [clothing]. They were teaching us about the history of Africa and I was really intrigued." During the assembly, however, a student named Frank Edgle opened the side auditorium door and yelled, "White power!" Suddenly, mayhem broke out as students jumped out of their seats and rummaged throughout the building looking for Edgle. "It was like someone ignited a huge barn burner match," described Val. "People started throwing things and students started running" in different directions, she explained. "People were being literally run over" as the uproar "spilled into the hallways." Anything people could get their hands on was used as a weapon. Trashcans were set on fire, Val said, and books and erasers were tossed around.

Gerald Wilson, then enrolled as a sophomore vocational student at McCaskey, was a member of the Black Student Union. "I was a participant in the Black History assembly," he said. He was supposed to perform that day. "All of the biggest black kids in the school were walking around in teams of six or eight looking for Frank Edgle." Crowds of black students approached white students in the hallways and asked, "Do you know where Frank Edgle is?" or "Are you one of his boys?"

Locked in fisticuffs, black and white students emptied onto Reservoir Street in front of the building. Clashes were scattered around the campus outside of the school as many frightened students waited for their buses and others tried to reach their cars. Charles Hatfield, a sixteen-year-old white student, and Dale Quigley, a seventeen-year-old milk deliveryman, were beaten so badly that they were rushed to the hospital. Quigley, who had just left a nearby restaurant after having lunch, was assailed by fifteen black students and was left in critical condition before Officer Kenneth Bomberger rushed through the crowd to rescue him. Quigley was placed in the intensive care unit for rib injuries. Meanwhile, Officer Bomberger was treated for injuries that he suffered in the melee. Reports in the local newspapers indicated that at least sixteen others were treated for minor cuts and bruises at the school's infirmary.[12]

Nancy Val became an unlucky victim of the violence. "I remember walking with my books heading for home, until my cousin told me we could get a ride from one of her friends," Val said. "As we walked toward the car I could see a group of about fifty African American women on the field in front of McCaskey. I tried not to make eye contact, but I knew they were waiting for a fight." Suddenly, Val was attacked and knocked unconscious. "When I awoke a couple of minutes later, I saw an African American male named Larry [Martin], [who] happened to be the captain of the basketball team, pulling these women off me and my cousin." Moments later the ambulance arrived and took Val to the hospital to be treated for cracked ribs and a concussion. "It was one of the most unforgettable days of my life."[13]

Reinforcements from the state police appeared at McCaskey by 1:00 p.m., and by 1:30 p.m., twenty off-duty officers had arrived. Authorities arrested five students and one adult for the rioting. The adult was Benjamin Bethea, who, at age twenty-one, was there with several Black Arise members to support the Black Student Union. The police charged him with, according to the *Lancaster New Era*, "encouraging and inciting an unlawful threat to take the life and do bodily harm to school officials and students." The hearing for Bethea was set for 10:00 a.m. on Monday, November 11.

School was closed for the remainder of the day. Maintenance workers spent that afternoon removing painted phrases—"White Power" and "Black Power"—and several obscenities from the sidewalks and exterior of the building. The chief of police ordered his officers to limit large groups from forming throughout the city. At 2:00 p.m., a group estimated to consist of between fifty and one hundred people that gathered in front of the Higbee Elementary School at the corner of South Duke and Chester Streets in the Seventh Ward were ordered to disperse by city police. The *Lancaster New Era* article about the melee featured an image of an unidentified white student who had his shirt ripped off and was being ushered to safety by elderly men.

Later that evening, Lancaster City School Board president John E. Hambright announced "all city schools would be closed" the following day. He asked district teachers to report to work for meetings about the situation. "The city's youth," declared Hambright, "must realize that the schools are here for one purpose—their education! Those who want an education can come. But those students who are intent upon disrupting the school schedule and apparently are more interested in leading uprisings … they'll have to stay out." He avowed, "That's the policy of the board." Hambright's comments were directed toward Edgle and those who rioted, but in the Seventh Ward, African Americans sensed that the words were aimed at them. The comments struck a nerve.

The following day, Friday, November 1, school was canceled as school district officials met to resolve the problem. High school principal John Rodman said that he was surprised by the "speed with which Negro young people, whom I know as fine students, just, well, exploded, the way they did."[14] Lancaster's NAACP president Rev. Ernest Christian was invited to address the faculty regarding the concerns of the African American students. He reported that many black students felt that some teachers "were prejudiced against them."[15] Christian suggested that the school district make an effort to employ more minority teachers. It was a heated discussion. Several teachers defended themselves, arguing that "racial unrest has been brewing at McCaskey for several years" and saying that the blame should be directed at the "lack of discipline, especially in the hallways and during lunch periods." Patrick Kenney, director of the Lancaster County Human Relations Commission, jumped into the dialogue. He claimed the problem was deeply entrenched in the dynamics of the city. "We've got to eliminate the white man's fear of the black neighborhood, and we've got to remove the black man's fear of certain white neighborhoods." Edward Allen, executive director of the Urban League of Lancaster County, said, "Ninety-five percent of the black population of this area is concentrated in the southeast area," the Seventh Ward. "Such a condition as this should not exist." "It is an old cliché," Allen continued, "but the one about the family that works together, prays together, and plays together stays together can certainly be applied to a community."[16]

It was an explosive twenty-four hours. In spite of that, one of the decisions was to have the school's football game against Steelton Highspire played as previously scheduled that Saturday at 1:30 p.m. It was a calculated risk, but the gathering of the entire community just two days after the disturbance at McCaskey presented a powder keg on the cusp of exploding.

The mood was already tense and confusing before the game kicked off. The school arranged to have extra police on duty. That hardly mattered to members of the black community, nearly forty-five in total, who showed up at the game, each carrying an umbrella. It was a gorgeous day: sunny and clear skies, and a gentle chill. The daunting multitude of teenagers and others in their early twenties brandishing umbrellas on one of the sunniest days of the fall struck wholesale panic among others in the crowd. They sat in separate areas of the visiting bleachers. Many of them crowded into the northern end of the stadium, while a larger group convened at the southern end.

As the national anthem played, none of the African American spectators stood. Not standing for the national anthem was fairly common after the 1968 Olympics. "We had rituals for everything," Benjamin Bethea admitted. "We would drink wine on the way up [to the game], and then we would save the bottles." Speaking for his friends in Black Arise, Bethea explained that his group would not allow other African Americans to stand up during the national anthem. "We would throw our empty bottles at black people" who acknowledged the American flag. "Everybody knew that you didn't [stand for the] pledge," said Bethea, "especially after John Carlos and Tommie Smith." Bethea considered standing for the pledge "a real Uncle Tom move."[17] No one was safe from the harassment. Some of Steelton Highspire's fans complained about being spat on or insulted by the two groups.

When the game started, there were twelve gray-shirted policemen positioned strategically around the stadium. Another twenty-five off-duty officers sat in the bleachers, anticipating a flare-up. Officer J. Donald Schaeffer was stationed at the stadium's northeast corner. Throughout the first half, the throng tried to intimidate Schaeffer. "I was the only one at that corner," he recalled. "They were shooting me with their umbrellas," he said, gesturing with his fingers pointing like a gun. Schaeffer only gazed back at the crowd. This exchange went on the entire first half.

Halftime brought a fresh portent of conflict. Bethea, who was just out on bail for the rioting that occurred two days earlier, had only recently arrived at the game and made his way to the large group of friends perched in the visitors' bleachers. The two groups then merged together and marched single file around the track, marching in front of the home bleachers, and then went back toward their seats on the visiting side. Several individuals in the group aimed their umbrellas at the cops as they crossed paths. According to Schaeffer, Alfred Bethea, Ben's younger brother, pointed his umbrella at the officer and said, "I'll shoot your white honky motherfucking ass!"[18]

Officer Schaeffer retorted, "Come over here and I'll shove that umbrella down your throat." Schaeffer and Bethea knew each other. For five years, Schaeffer had walked the beat in the Seventh Ward. It was an assignment that afforded him many rare relationships while in the police force. On this day, however, Schaeffer had much to fear.

Alfred Bethea and the entire contingent charged after Schaeffer. Suddenly, Schaeffer was "standing there with nothing but a wall of black." Called a "Black Mob" by the local newspaper, Bethea and the group surrounded Schaeffer. Suddenly fists were flying.[19] Schaeffer was knocked to the ground and poked at with several umbrellas. While Schaeffer was down, Ben Bethea kicked him in the face. Schaeffer remembers, "Ben took his size ten jump boot and kicked me in the head, and out went my lights." As this happened, Alfred ran onto the middle of the field, took off his shirt, and provoked anyone in the crowd to challenge him to a fight.[20] He was chased off the field by the authorities.

After three minutes, police restrained Ben Bethea when one officer knocked him on his head with a nightstick and another sprayed him with mace. "They had a different kind of mace," Bethea mentioned. "It would make your face peel." Officers wearing blue riot helmets escorted him across the north end of the football field. This image appeared on the front page of the newspaper the following morning. As Bethea was led away in handcuffs, his chin was proudly elevated to the sky. He admitted, "We never let anyone see us hang our heads."[21] As Bethea was escorted away, his allies ran after in attempt to rescue him. Several officers from various sections of the sidelines converged. The rescue attempt was thwarted, but umbrellas flailed in the air and more punches were thrown at the cops. Police Chief David Rineer recovered one of the umbrellas, its handle knocked off and its shaft bent. More arrests were made on the football field. The arrested persons were rushed off the field and placed in a paddy wagon.

In all, eight policemen and a police cadet were injured during the melee. Several sustained injuries severe enough to be identified by the local newspaper. Police officers Schaeffer and Jerold Highfield were admitted to Lancaster General Hospital with serious head injuries. Lieutenant John Ulrich, as well as officers Eric Hjelm and Kenneth Miller, were placed on bed rest with leg and chest injuries.[22]

Bethea gave a significantly different version of the event. He maintained that the riot was caused by the police officers who lingered near the black spectators for the entire first half, subtly provoking them. As halftime neared its end, Bethea obstinately explained, "Someone told me my brother was getting beat up by police." He rushed out of his seat and found his brother restrained by officers behind the bleachers. There, Bethea and Officer Schaeffer met fisticuffs. "When I got there, the police[man] was sitting on top of [Alfred]," Bethea remembers. "I kicked [the cop] in the head." Several others jumped into the fray.[23] "The next thing I knew I was at the police station," Bethea said. He was charged with assaulting Officer

Schaeffer by "kicking him and striking him with an unknown blunt object" and Officer Highfield by "striking him about the head with an unknown blunt object." Bail for Bethea was set at $25,000.[24] Several other Seventh Ward adults were arrested for taking part in the riot. Nathaniel J. Dorsey, Will Boyer, and Terry Boyer were each charged with aggravated assault and battery of a police officer, and taking part in a fray. Five high school students were charged and then committed to Barnes Hall, a juvenile detention center near the city's southeast.[25]

As the media covered what had transpired on Thursday, October 31, and Saturday, November 2, the city appeared in unmistakable turmoil, and the School District of Lancaster was exposed as an institution that had failed to adapt to a changing reality, namely that nonwhites living in segregated parts of Lancaster had grown more and more disillusioned about the nation they lived in. The first African American assistant football coach at McCaskey High School, Fred Reed, admitted that "tensions were rising in Lancaster city" for months before these incidents. Reed, who had graduated from Franklin and Marshall College, Class of 1958, confessed that he was aware of "a group of individuals in the city who were very actively promoting black involvement and black power." Reed and Bethea were acquaintances. "I knew Ben very well," said Reed. "I taught him in junior high. And Ben and I had a lot of talks. We did not always see eye to eye, but from my perspective I thought Ben respected me, even though he did not always agree with me."[26]

Not many in Lancaster were left immune to the explosive episodes that occurred in the fall of 1968 at McCaskey High School. High school students, college students, and community members were all impacted. It appeared that Benjamin Bethea was the conduit from one end of the city to the other. "Ben was always interested in what had happened to African American people and was always interested in trying to do something about it," a reflective Reed indicated years later. "I always thought Ben was a really smart guy ... athletic and had leadership ability."

At first, people in Lancaster thought black power was a disorganized criminal faction within the civil rights struggle that was guided by young thugs who had acquired nominal education. However, the events of 1968 showed that race liberation was not at all part of the civil rights struggle. Rather, black power was a campaign led by intelligent, yet cynical and proud, leaders. Most were from the poorest part of the city and willing to take bold risks with the law. Some were college students; on campuses was where the idea of black power had its genesis. Together, townies and students worked to empower and reeducate Lancaster's black citizens in ways that frightened many people. And owing to the era's antipathy of authority, violence was on a hair trigger. Whereas the fall semester of the 1968–1969 school year concentrated on events in the city, Black Arise's central focus during the spring semester was on events at Franklin and Marshall College.

Chapter 7
THE BLACK STUDIES PROPOSAL

B EFORE THE POT boiled over on campus as it had in the city after the Martin Luther King assassination, the faculty of Franklin and Marshall College attempted to suppress the racial tension by hearing proposals for a black studies interdisciplinary field. In the spring of 1968, senior Afro-American Society member Lew Myers had initiated the venture when he circulated a memo to the chairpersons of each academic department asking about the probability of offering courses dealing with black studies. Many were receptive. Concerned faculty members made arrangements to work with Myers and several members of the Afro-American Society to sketch out a plan. Everybody was eager, and immediately formed the Curriculum Committee on the Black Studies Proposal to begin the process of creating the interdisciplinary program with a target of implementing it as an academic minor in the fall semester.[1] The concerned faculty included a representative each from the history, English, sociology, psychology, philosophy, and anthropology departments. LeRoy Pernell, Robert Lopatin, and Lew Thrash were the representatives from the Afro-American Society on the committee. O. W. Lacy, the college's dean of students, and Lew Myers, who was graduating in May and planned to remain on campus the following school year since he had accepted a job in the Office of Special Programs, were also on the curriculum committee.

For African American students at Franklin and Marshall, the creation of the Black Studies Department was of the utmost importance. LeRoy Pernell explained, "A black studies program can serve as a provider of tools for those whose interest may lie in the area of addressing themselves to the combatting [*sic*] of racism." But why a separate department dedicated to African American literature, history, and art? Why an interdisciplinary approach dealing with the cultural, economic, and social aspects of the black experience in America? "The answer lies in a true understanding of purpose," Pernell said. He cleverly explained with a strong line of reasoning, "A black studies department should concern itself with providing the students with information helpful in guiding [them] towards the areas necessary in order to develop methods needed to challenge and defeat practices that have been in existence for hundreds of years." Pernell suggested that white students needed to understand the "total facts concerning the black experience," including making a realistic examination of the urban slums and all the things produced by segregation, like schoolchildren without lunch money, what it felt like to be forced to sit in the back of the bus, unwarranted police searches, ominous glares upon entering lavish department stores, violent attacks and bombings on homes and churches, young students trekking miles to get to the only black school available, and much more. The desired "black studies department, as opposed to selecting courses in various departments," Pernell argued, "offers the student the coordination through specialization that he needs" to relate to the African American perspective. "The black experience is of such a nature that it is unlike any other experience," was Pernell's analysis of the issue.[2] His ultimate argument was that Franklin and Marshall could not call itself a liberal arts college with the goal of preparing its students to seek knowledge concerning their own existence and the existence of others until an interdisciplinary black studies academic field became a reality.

Many of the concerned faculty on the curriculum committee felt that Franklin and Marshall was not yet ready for the program. Most of their doubts were of their own professional competence to advise the black studies department. Some suggested they wait instead of rushing into a program.

The professors' suggestion carried much weight in the committee's final decision. Just before the students and faculty left for summer break in May 1968, the curriculum committee announced that there would be no black studies department come the fall. With backing from the dean of students, the committee decided it would take two to three years to implement a comprehensive interdisciplinary program. So the committee offered a typical academic alternative by urging individual departments to offer courses in literature, history, sociology, psychology, art, and religion pertaining to black culture— just the thing Pernell argued against.

The announcement was a heavy blow to the Afro-American Society, who saw the decision as the college's way of dodging the issue. With the help of Lew Myers, the students, however, did not waver. Myers spent his first summer after graduation writing curriculum for a three-credit multidisciplinary class involving multiple disciplines and several professors. "As I envision it," Myers rationalized, "the object of this course would be to give the students some idea of what it is like to be black and live in America."[3] He sent his proposal to the Franklin and Marshall faculty on August 27, 1968. In early September, he met with eight department chairmen to discuss his course.

Myers's proposed course was called Black Reality. To date, he said, "there is no Black history course; the American Literature course includes no Black authors; American history courses only discuss Black people in their role as slaves; the Sociology Department never offered its Race and Ethnic Relations course ... My point is clear." Another point was to be made: as the 1968–1969 school year approached, the college had just two professors who were African American. Myers suggested that the perception of Franklin and Marshall by African Americans outside the college was that it was "brainwashing and assimiliat[ing]" black students into the established culture. "Personally," he said, "I do not hold that view[,] but I do find it hard to convince other blacks not associated with Franklin and Marshall." He concluded that it would benefit the college at large to implement his proposed course.

Myers's drafted curriculum was quite impressive. His course's thesis centered on explaining what it was like for an African American to live in the United States. To articulate this, Myers wanted students to experience firsthand what it was like to live in underdeveloped and impoverished urban areas. He wanted enrollees to gain an insight into how African Americans were treated by the criminal justice system. His Black Reality curriculum demanded that students spend time in Lancaster's seventh ward. In addition, he offered an intense reading list that included Stokely Carmichael's *Black Power*, Malcolm X's autobiography, John Howard Griffin's *Black Like Me*, W. E. B. Du Bois's *Philadelphia Negro*, Martin Luther King's *Why We Can't Wait*, Ralph Ellison's *Invisible Man*, Charles Eric Lincoln's *Is Anybody Listening to Black America?*, and several works by James Baldwin.

He also thought the class should feature guest speakers, pop quizzes, and a term paper. His curriculum did not include a midterm or final exam.[4]

The Franklin and Marshall faculty were enthusiastic about Myers's class. He inspired action by two departments, History and Religion, which announced the creation of respective black studies courses. The History Department created a class entitled The Negro and Reform, while the Religion Department offered White Racism and Black Churches. Myers's Black Reality course was undertaken by eight concerned faculty members and altered into an interdepartmental course called the Black Experience in America.

Some considered modifications to Myers's curriculum short-term successes, seeing Franklin and Marshall as making a concerted effort to cease racial misunderstanding. While proponents considered the three courses instruments for recruiting more multiracial students, the Afro-American Society rebuffed the administration's decision. LeRoy Pernell, one of the college's first outspoken critics, responded with a feisty admonition. The campus newspaper printed Pernell's scathing letter to the editor. "These courses have no real meaningful purpose in revolutionizing the White mind and have even less of a relevance to the education of the Black student." Pernell called the History Department's Negro and Reform course an "absurdity." Referencing the course's title, he called a Negro a "mythical bastard," saying that for the "true Afro-American there has been no meaningful reform." Black people, he contended, "are still as oppressed as in 1860; only the physical chains are missing." Speaking about the Religion Department's White Racism and Black Churches in America course, Pernell became more shrill. He suggested that the title was the only thing interesting, especially considering that Franklin and Marshall did not have a professor qualified to speak about the black church.

"This course would perhaps be relevant," he remarked, "if it dealt with the racist attitude and the history of Churchanity, as opposed to Christianity, in the White Church."[5]

Pernell charged, in his last argument, the Black Experience in America course with hypocrisy. He tossed out a question: "Why this study of the Black man's thoughts and feelings as if he were a museum piece to be studied and discerned as to its function?" He answered his own question as follows, feigning indignation.

> There is no need for this. The problem is not there. Don't examine us, we're not the sick ones. The illness is in your society. The illness is in you. The oppression comes from White society. Blacks are not the reason for Black oppression. If you are really looking for the source of racism, examine your own society. If this course is truly to mean anything, it should be entitled *The White Experience in America.*

Many years later, Pernell, who would become dean of the Florida A&M Law School, explained that his consternation over the Black Experience in America course was a matter of black students having a voice on campus. He wanted Lew Myers's Black Reality course offered without any alterations made by white faculty members.[6]

Just days after Pernell's piece appeared in the campus newspaper, students started firing back and defending the three courses. David Katz's letter to the editor took no side steps in answering many of Pernell's indictments. "May I suggest to LeRoy Pernell that he take— or at least audit—some of these courses that he finds so absurd or irrelevant." Katz readily admitted, "These courses may, indeed, turn out to be 'pretty pink white liberal' courses," yet, he argued, "they may be beneficial in helping correct what you would correctly term 'the white problem' (i.e., the black revolution and white racism)."[7]

Katz and several white students were especially supportive of the Black Experience in America course.

Lew Myers entered the debate from his job with the Office of Special Programs. Since the faculty had adapted his proposed Black Reality course, Myers now had reservations regarding what the administration was planning. He protested, "The original notion was definitely what I would call a Black-oriented course and it would definitely have offered something for the black student in particular, but as it came down it was more an informational course for white people." Myers, it turned out, spent the end of the fall 1968 semester persuading black students not to enroll in the course. He later remarked, "I kept telling them that the course is not what it was going to be. It would not be a course for black students as much as an informative course for white students."[8]

As registration for the spring semester commenced in November 1968, only one of the three courses was offered as planned. To the dismay of the History and Religion Departments, their respective courses were canceled. This blow was especially hard for concerned faculty who'd already lost the trust of a number of Afro-American Society members. Myers's adapted interdisciplinary class remained on the course list, however. Leaflets were distributed throughout campus to advertise the course. It read as follows:

> This course seeks to present a balanced and objective account of the forces affecting the lives of Black Americans and to give the student insight into the feelings, thoughts and contributions of Black Americans in this society. The course is open to all students.[9]

Officially, the course was called Interdepartmental-4: The Black Experience in America, and it was advertised as an experimental class. One of the course's professors called it "an ad hoc venture."[10] Anthropology professor Adebisi Otudeko volunteered to coordinate the class. Seven other professors—each earnestly serious about being part of making changes regarding racial understanding—shared duties teaching the course. Their disciplines ranged from history to anthropology, sociology to government, and economics to psychology. The diversity of the group can be debated. Otudeko was born in Nigeria and arrived at Franklin and Marshall in 1966. First-year sociology professor Murli Sinha was from India. Six other professors were white, and all male, including Leon Galis, assistant professor of philosophy; Sidney Wise, professor of government and chairman of the department; Louis Athey, assistant professor of history; Donald J. Tyrrell, second-year assistant professor of psychology; Thomas Glenn, assistant professor of economics; and Gerald E. Enscoe, associate professor of English. All of the professors taught the course pro bono. Each instructor except for Otudeko carried a full academic load in addition to his commitment to the Interdepartmental-4 course. And they were responsible for leading three to four sessions each.[11] Only Otudeko was required to attend every session. It must be noted that irregular attendance by the other professors ultimately created one of the largest inconsistencies for the course.

The Interdepartmental-4 course caused a lot of debate among the fifty-eight African American students on campus. Members of the Afro-American Society were split. Benjamin Bowser, the Society's president in 1968 when the course was under negotiation, came out against the class. He never could grasp how the college could offer such a class while treating it like all of F&M's other courses. Bowser believed the class would be black studies in name only. He argued that a black studies course should be more than academic: "It requires fieldwork," he said. "It requires engagement with kids.

It requires comparative perspective."[12] His opposition was based on a number of factors. Bowser felt that the professors on campus were not qualified to instruct the class, that they did not understand what African Americans experienced every day in America. He was very skeptical of the course's basic design. Bowser wanted the course's classroom to be the Seventh Ward, where the daily routines of black Americans could be studied up close. Instead, it became clear to him that the course evolved into something that would have greater value for white students. At a meeting of the Afro-American Society, Bowser presented his argument, claiming that the course was a big mistake. He contended that black students "would be used as exhibits A, B, and C, while the white students would gain a great deal from the class [and] walk away with As, and [black students] would walk away with Cs."[13] His argument was costly to sustaining his position as Society president.

At the time, most of the members of the Afro-American Society were younger than Bowser. They felt that their leader had to be more aggressive, even more radical. They wanted the class, believing that it was going to be a subjective approach "to provide them with a personal enlightenment about their own lives and the part that blackness plays in their role in society."[14] Lew Thrash, who supported the college's decision to create the course, emerged as the next president of the Society.

When the dust settled, and after Thrash had defeated Bowser in the election of president of the Afro-American Society, students began registering for their spring courses. However, the final enrollment in the Interdepartmental-4 course may have scored a postelection victory for Bowser. When the class held its first meeting in February 1969, there were forty-nine students enrolled. Just twelve of those were African American, including Thrash.[15] An unpredictable semester was dawning.

Chapter 8

THE FISHBOWL

    THE 1969 SPRING semester at many colleges across the country got off to a rough start. In January alone, at least seven universities experienced black student militancy. San Francisco State was in the middle of a five-month takeover, beginning on November 6, 1968, and ending on March 20, 1969. At Brandeis University in Massachusetts, about sixty-four members of the Afro-American Society took over Ford Hall, which housed the college's switchboard room and several classrooms. For eleven days, students occupied the building while waiting for their demands to be met by the college's administration. Near Philadelphia, Pennsylvania, twenty black students and a few nonstudents at Swarthmore College barricaded themselves inside the admissions office for eight days, which ended abruptly when college president Dr. Courtney Smith died of a heart attack.[1] Swarthmore graduate Fania Davis and recent Franklin and Marshall graduate Sam Jordan, the latter of whom was at the time undergoing his appeal of the May 1968 charges of possessing a gun and bombing the Lancaster Selective Service office, were on campus during the Swarthmore disturbance. The couple were, at the time, avowed Communists with a trip to Cuba on the docket.[2] Swarthmore administrators accused Davis and Jordan of inciting the occupation, though it was never proven that the couple played any role at all in the takeover. Other takeovers or strikes occurred that month at Minnesota, Pittsburgh, Wilberforce, and California–Berkeley. In February, twenty-four-hour takeovers occurred at Duke and Rutgers. Every demonstration of black militancy shared common demands: an increase in faculty diversity, the creation of programs that would increase the number of black students on campus, and the implementation of black studies programs.

These episodes placed Franklin and Marshall's administration under the gun. Anticipation over the impending Interdepartmental-4: The Black Experience in America course finally ended on February 3, 1969, when the class convened for the first time. Professor Otudeko showed the CBS documentary film (starring Bill Cosby) *Black History: Lost, Stolen, or Strayed*, followed by a lecture from Leon Galis and a panel discussion that included Lew Myers, Professor Louis Athey, and Professor Sidney Wise. Thereafter, the course was scheduled to meet twice a week for three total hours per week. There would be a total of twenty-one class meetings. Additionally, three times throughout the semester, the course's professors programmed mandatory evening panel discussions aimed at tying up the lesson materials presented during previous class meetings. All of this was listed on the daunting syllabus that Professor Otudeko distributed on that first day of class. The syllabus that the eight professors constructed was an overt deviation from Lew Myers's proposed Black Reality reading list. From the looks of it, the professors planned a semester full of discussions about history and philosophy, not debates and observations focusing on contemporary concerns about race.

Lessons led by Professors Galis, Wise, Tyrrell, and Athey were lecture-based, whereas Enscoe, Sinha, and Glenn designed their classes Socratically. Otudeko meanwhile sat in on every class meeting and facilitated the course. Each professor had two weeks to teach his three or four ninety-minute lessons. No matter who was leading the session, the Socratic practice or note-taking abilities were not heavily weighted in the final grade.[3]

Galis's, Wise's, Tyrrell's, and Athey's discussions focused on popular essays, theories, and readings taken from historical works, black literature, child psychology, and philosophy that complemented important civil rights issues since the Civil War. For example, philosophy professor Leon Galis used John Stuart Mill's essay *On Liberty* as the text for his three sessions, during which he attempted to prove that the racial crises of the late 1960s exposed a "deep inconsistency in liberalism." Galis contended that if his theory held true, then the failure of the successive liberal presidential administrations of Kennedy and Johnson to solve the problems of the poor, the young, and the black might be the result, in his words, "not of their failure to be liberal enough, but of inherent defects in the conception of society and social change embodied in the liberal tradition itself."[4] In retrospect, Galis's lectures may have been too advanced for the students. He later admitted, "The material I worked up would have been more appropriate for an advanced seminar."[5]

Whereas Galis's presentations were formal lectures that allowed few questions, his colleague in the History Department, Louis Athey, presented four lectures in three class meetings centered on the general theme "Myths and Realities of the Black Experience." His lectures were titled "Docile Child or 'Freedom Fighter'"; "Black Reconstruction"; "'New Racism' and Segregation: Black Responses—Accommodation and Protest"; and "Myths and Realities in Black Protest Thought Since 1920." Each lecture was accompanied with a reading list that included works from Frank Tannenbaum, W. E. B. Du Bois, John Hope Franklin, Marcus Garvey, A. Philip Randolph, Malcolm X, Ralph Bunche, and Martin Luther King.

Galis's and Athey's colleague, Professor Donald J. Tyrrell, had Jonathan Kozol's *Death at an Early Age* on his reading list. Responsible for providing the psychological component of the course, Tyrrell centered his theme on racial awareness. By the end of his three meetings, he was hoping students would be able to discuss "how, and at what age, children begin to evaluate their own and other racial groups." The seemingly useful explanatory mechanism covered in his lectures was the self-fulfilling prophecy, which he described in the course syllabus "as the notion that an individual's values, beliefs, and expectations concerning the behavior of another individual will determine, to some extent, the actual behavior of that individual." Tyrrell said he hoped "to demonstrate its applicability to the intellectual and academic behavior of the minority group child." Tyrrell's lecture series was designed to get his students to see that "children do evaluate their own racial group, as well as others." He said, "The effects of the self-fulfilling prophecy are relevant to both inter[-] and intra-racial interactions."[6]

The fourth and final lecturer of the course was the college's award-winning government professor Sidney Wise. Professor Wise's three presentations concentrated on how the government tackled problems in black communities across the United States. The details of his three meetings were vague on the course syllabus.

The seminars of Professors Enscoe, Sinha, and Glenn, structured much like a graduate course, called on higher-level and analytical thinking from the undergraduate students, who were given a sizable reading list that was supposed to prepare them to perform intellectual exercises like, "Relate the negative evaluation of the Negro by both whites and blacks to socioeconomic status, and academic performance," or to do other things such as "choose" the topic of slavery, sharecropping, or the urban ghetto "and interpret it in terms of an 'institution of social control' and its impact upon the Black Experience in America."[7] The expectation was that each student read all of the material on the reading list before each seminar. Guest lecturers were invited to these seminars to share personal experiences in the freedom struggle, including one professor from Lincoln University, one of two historically black universities located in Pennsylvania, and others from Lancaster City. During three class meetings, black students who were enrolled at Franklin and Marshall, but not in the Interdepartmental-4 course, led sessions. None of those guest speakers were identified on the syllabus.[8]

From the start, the twelve African American students in the class were confused. At the first class meeting, Otudeko explained that the course was going to be a study of "philosophical discussions, literature, history, anthropology, psychology, sociology, government and economics." Looking around at each other, none of the students thought that method could have any relevance to their lives on top of that which can be learned in general elective courses. At the end of the semester, English professor Gerald Enscoe admitted, "To the extent that in announcing the new course, we led many of the blacks to assume that this was a course for them, we misrepresented it." It was now clear to all that the course was designed primarily to educate white students.[9]

During Professor Leon Galis's opening-day lecture, one student asked if a "white person could teach a black person anything about the 'black experience' in America." Galis, whose lecture was about classical liberalism, answered, "I obviously could not have the experience of a person who was black, but that I thought that the experience of being black was not absolutely necessary for understanding the point I was trying to make about the liberal tradition in political philosophy." It was during this student–professor exchange that Galis made a comment that would come back to haunt him. He remarked, "I would have to rely on the black students in the course as 'resource persons.'"[10]

Resource persons. It was an unfortunate choice of phrase, one that placed the black students on the same level as the professors. The comment indicated that white students would get more out of the course than the black students. Instead of cleaning up the mess, Galis dug deeper. He asked the African American students to "tell it like it is," because, he said, the "white professors could not really interpret the experience of being Black in America."[11] Galis was admitting his ineptitude. Yet he was not alone. According to Professor Enscoe, "At least three of us admitted our own incompetence." At that inaugural session, the "Black students were encouraged from the first to believe that they were already experts in much of the subject matter of the course." Professor Enscoe conceded that the African American students were encouraged to remain in the course "primarily because they were needed, that without their contributions the course would not be a success."[12]

Speaking to the students on that first day, Galis was eager to, even confident about his ability to, provide useful observations about various aspects of race in America. He grew up in Athens, Georgia, double majored in philosophy and psychology as an undergraduate at the University of Georgia, and earned a doctorate in philosophy from the University of North Carolina paid for by the National Defense Education Act Fellowship. But it was as a student at Georgia that he witnessed firsthand the courage that civil rights workers needed to possess. He sat in the audience in 1961 when then attorney general

Robert F. Kennedy, during his Law Day address at the university, put the state on notice that the Kennedy administration fully intended to enforce federal civil rights laws. "I joined in the vigorous applause," Galis, looking back on that time, remembers. On another occasion, Galis had been meeting with a professor "a couple floors up from the entrance" to the University of Georgia's Registrar's Office, he recalled, when Charlayne Hunter and Hamilton Holmes "were escorted through a howling mob to enroll, by federal court order," in the university."[13] He noted, "The tear gas had been deployed to disperse a mob, which took exception to the presence of Ms. Hunter in one of the women's dorms I had to pass by to get to the library." Admittedly, Galis was not an activist in the sense that he joined in the demonstrations. But he always remained in "slack-jawed awe" of what Hunter, Holmes, and countless others "endured for the sake of what we're all due as Americans."

Galis had arrived in Lancaster in the sixties having never laid eyes on a northern city. He grew up in a southern town chock-full of antebellum mansions and open space. Clearly, the environs of Lancaster County were foreign to him and his wife, Diana. However, as a professor he was sharp and quick-witted. He was valued as an educator at Franklin and Marshall from the moment he arrived on campus. He taught courses that ranged all over the Philosophy Department's curriculum, including moral philosophy, logic, philosophy of religion, and political philosophy, and a Nietzsche seminar. Galis had just received the Christian R. and Mary F. Lindback Foundation Award for Distinguished Teaching. He rode the momentum into a volunteer position as an Interdepartmental-4 instructor that spring.[14]

Galis thought the interdisciplinary course was a good idea. In fact, he called it a "pretty good course." Admittedly, however, he wished that his colleagues had named it something different. "The main thing wrong with it was the title," he remarked years later. "There was no way [six] white guys, an African, and an Indian could say anything credible about the black experience in America."[15] Notwithstanding the conclusive blunder, the eight professors did possess talents that could contribute to the discussion about race in America during the 1960s.

If there was an Interdepartmental-4 faculty member whom students trusted the most, it would have been "Gerry" Enscoe. Enscoe's students, black and white alike, revered him. Louis Butcher, an English major who graduated in 1965, years later remembered Enscoe as a "good guy." Butcher recalled, "We met in his home. He'd serve wine, [and] guys would sit [around]. Teaching a black history course would fit him. I know I felt very comfortable with Gerry."[16] Enscoe was one of the architects of the Pre-College Enrichment Program, having served as director during its inaugural summer in 1964. Throughout the sixties, Enscoe seemed to be the radical representative on the faculty, often involved with or supporting activism. In 1966, he challenged the campus president over the legitimacy of student radicalism. When Franklin and Marshall president Keith Spalding claimed that many universities had been "ruined by radical activity," Enscoe boldly responded by giving a lecture at a student–faculty forum in which he said that radicals on campus are "more important to the process of learning than a good library." He was an active member of the Lancaster Peace Committee, for which he organized supporters off campus. Enscoe led a petition drive expressing opposition to the Vietnam War, hoping to rally other college professors to do the same. To students, he called the Vietnam War "stupid and insane." One student remembered seeing Enscoe at a Ban the Bomb rally in Lancaster City "right there in front of the group!"[17] In 1966, Enscoe was an organizer of the Lancaster chapter of National Citizens for Kennedy–Fulbright. The nationwide organization was made up of liberal Democrats who opposed the Johnson administration's foreign policy and wanted to see the president replaced by the Kennedy scion.

Enscoe's high-impact rapport with students typically kept interests at a peak. However, for a campus in a fit of racial confusion, the Interdepartmental-4 class became a thumb in the eye. As the semester proceeded, formal class presentations or simple responses during class discussion tended to focus on students' personal experiences without reference to the required reading listed on the syllabus. But not all of the students in the class sensed the confusion. Brett Harwood, a white sophomore, suggested that there were "some heated arguments in the class[, but] none of the black students ever voiced dissatisfaction aside from unhappiness over the name of the course."[18] No one outside of the Afro-American Society knew that there were major problems fostering. There were signs nonetheless.

After several weeks, many of the black students began asking questions as to whether or not they should remain in the class. Professor Enscoe encouraged them to stay, not because they would miss out on an exceptional learning experience, but "because they were needed." The professors started to give their black students teaching responsibilities. Enscoe admitted, "One of my periods in literature I turned over to a panel of four blacks in order to present a black sensibility responding to the work of black writers, and apparently one or two [other professors] did something similar." When Enscoe's panel session ended, one of his students turned to him and said, "How much are we going to get paid for doing this?" Still, Enscoe and his colleagues failed to catch on to the sense that a portion of their students felt like rats in a maze.

When midsemester grades were reported, the black students learned they were receiving the lowest grades in the class. Those in the course griped to their friends, "Look at my grade. Isn't this a shitty grade?"[19] Four students were placed on warning of failing the course, while four others maintained C-minus averages. Irrationally, some students shut down. Their participation in the class decreased and their attendance became irregular. Other students panicked. Each of the twelve black students in the course was under intense academic pressure. They were afraid that their college career was in jeopardy with a poor grade in the Interdepartmental-4 course. Others feared the ominous Vietnam War draft if they struggled academically or simply failed out of college, as local draft boards took class rank into consideration when preparing draft calls.[20]

There was some grumbling among the students. One contended the class was an example of "'whitey using the nigger' for his own purposes."[21] Before class and after, sometimes when bumping into one another on campus, some of the Interdepartmental-4 students casually voiced their frustrations to the professors. The faculty dismissed the complaints. Professor Enscoe conceded, "We tended to downplay them, to argue that they were wrong to feel this way, that we were doing something valuable and appreciate[d] their help."[22]

Despite the carping among students, not a single formal complaint was ever filed about the class. Professor Leon Galis astutely sensed something was amiss by the spring recess. In April, LeRoy Pernell approached him about enrolling in the course. Since the course was fairly well along, Galis did not come right out and say yes. Pernell gave Galis the impression that the course was "regarded as a moderate success" but that his friends felt like they were in a "'fish bowl,' that they were being peered at and scrutinized like case studies." Pernell continued, saying that the class "as a whole was too 'theoretical' and should be more 'practical' and more 'action-oriented.'" The two discussed the likelihood of incorporating firsthand experiences that taught about political reform, urban rehabilitation, and economic reforms. Galis agreed with Pernell's suggestions, but he explained why it would be difficult for "a small undergraduate college to do[,] since it required people with highly specialized knowledge who were in woefully short supply."[23] Galis advised Pernell to see Professor Otudeko about late enrollment into the course. He better suggested that Pernell should help rewrite the course's curriculum for the following school year. Pernell was in the middle of leading the Afro-American Society in an effort to implement its own urban rehabilitation and economic reform programs in the Seventh Ward. He said that although he would like to help the college rewrite the curriculum, he was "too deeply involved in the development of the Society's program to do both."[24] Galis failed to see this as a complaint. Things only got worse once the students returned from spring break.

The big topic of conversation among the students during the second half of the semester was what had just occurred at Cornell University. On the morning of April 19, the start of Parents' Weekend on the Ithaca campus, about forty members of the Afro-American Society occupied Willard Straight Hall. The protestors evicted parents and all the employees from the building, seizing control of the campus radio station. They were demanding a change in the "racist attitudes" maintained by the Ivy League college's administration and campus police, as well as the lack of relevant black studies courses.[25] After the protestors engaged in a physical confrontation with white students from Delta Upsilon, two bundles of guns, including sixteen rifles and three shotguns, along with ammunition belts, were delivered to the students occupying Willard Straight Hall. The weapons were to be used for self-defense only. Later that night, as police cruisers where circling the building, several dozen members of Cornell's chapter of Students for a Democratic Society, in an act of support of the black students, formed a phalanx around Willard Straight Hall. After thirty-six hours, the students, now numbering eighty, finally walked out of the building. Two occupiers were photographed clutching rifles and shotguns and wearing bandoliers. The takeover ended only after Cornell's vice president and vice provost agreed to sign a seven-part agreement that provided amnesty for every demonstrator, granted dismissal of disciplinary proceedings stemming from past demonstrations, agreed to university responsibility for any damage done to Willard Straight Hall during the protest, provided university legal defense against any civil suits that might ensue from the sit-in, and provided twenty-four-hour guarding of the college's Afro-American Center.

As imagined, within days, the incident at Cornell led to similar actions taken up by students at other institutions of higher learning. This time, black students at Harvard University and a mix of black and Puerto Rican students at the City College of New York (CCNY) effected strikes on their respective campuses. Media coverage of each student-led disturbance was ubiquitous and often subjective. Most outlets compared the students to Cuban revolutionaries, especially when expounding the presence of weapons. *New York Times* columnist Tom Wicker opined, "The widely distributed photograph of black students at Cornell carrying their rifles and shotguns out of a building they had seized may well be the most shocking evidence yet—at least to white people—of the extent to which the American people have been divided into hostile, nearly warring forces."[26] Two days after the Cornell takeover, and one day after the incidents at Harvard and CCNY, Democratic senator of West Virginia Robert C. Byrd introduced a campus disorder bill "to provide imprisonment and fines for demonstrators who interfered with the operations of any school receiving federal funds."[27] Certainly, this image, along with the violence that followed the assassination of Martin Luther King and the news of urban riots in Newark, Washington, and Detroit, introduced to the country two frightening realities: (1) that black college students had connected their struggle in the academic environment with those people who struggled in the inner city, and (2) that black students were heeding the social revitalization philosophy of the Black Panther Party that professed armed self-defense to improve their lot. This is not to mean that Afro-American Society members at Franklin and Marshall College thought it was a good idea to place guns under their beds in their dorm rooms. But it was certainly a topic of conversation at Afro Hall. The attitude of African Americans at F&M grew cynical, even on a campus where progress was being made.

On April 30, a study guide that included thirteen questions was distributed to the students in the Black Experience in America course. Seven of the questions, Professor Otudeko said, would appear on the final exam. The puzzled students looked around at each other. Some rolled their eyes; others shrugged their shoulders. They brooded, "Are we really being forced to take a final?"[28]

More bad news was probably not what the students had in mind. On the morning of Wednesday, May 21, the students picked up graded term papers, a required assignment listed on the syllabus. The grades of the black students ranged from A to D. If the faculty felt comfortable enough to allow the black students to lead sessions and talk about their own experiences, the students complained, then how could the professors give them Ds while the white students in the class received As?

The professor who represented the students' major graded the term papers. Each term paper was assessed according to Franklin and Marshall's traditional standards of grading papers, such as mastery of research, how the information was presented, implementation of footnotes, and the extent to which traditional academic concepts were followed. Interdepartmental-4 students were required to complete assigned readings and write a research paper based on any aspect of the black experience in the United States. Lew Myers impartially acknowledged, "Some of the kids turned in seven to eight pages of stuff off the top of their heads, an editorial."[29] Professor Enscoe expressed that his African American students submitted "personal testaments," not "legitimate piece[s] of research."[30] Enscoe commented on students' lack of citations and references to assigned readings. Criticisms from the other professors included, "This is an editorial, no books, no sources" and "You have not dealt with the topic."[31] The students had turned in diatribes about their own experiences in the United States. "I know one kid got something like an A over C," recounted Lew Myers, "an A for content but a C because he didn't do what was asked. Therefore," he said in conclusion, that particular student received "a B."[32] Whether it was premeditated or the scores on the term papers was the final straw, the students that afternoon decided to protest the forthcoming final exam.

Afro Hall buzzed with dissention that evening, Even in 1969, before social networking, it did not take long for word to spread at a small college like Franklin and Marshall. Lew Thrash and his eleven peers who were enrolled in the Interdepartmental-4 course began brainstorming with their Afro-American Society peers for ways to voice their grievances to the professors. "That's when the proverbial shit hit the fan," recalls Benjamin Bowser, who was not enrolled in the course but was present at the meeting. "Instead of this being something that brought the campus together, [the course] was a bomb right in the middle of race relations on the campus."[33] It took the students just hours to create their plan.

The professors' insensitivity is arguably defensible. Evidence shows that the crux of the black students' opposition included traditional academic practices, not just their particular demands for the Interdepartmental-4 class. The professors were under the impression that they had a bunch of students who were only upset at their grades on course work. It makes sense that there was confusion between the two parties.

Beyond the classroom, turmoil was about to engulf Franklin and Marshall College. At 4:00 p.m., Professor Otudeko received a telephone call from Afro-American Society president Lew Thrash. Operating as the students' spokesperson, Thrash said that he and his peers would like to meet with him before he left campus for the night. Otudeko agreed. Moments later, five black students, including Thrash, arrived at Otudeko's office in Goethean Hall. Only one of the five was not enrolled in the course. The students insisted that there should not be a comprehensive exam and said that all of the black students enrolled in the class would prevent the professors from administering a final. Otudeko calmly told them to put their feelings in writing, saying that he would present their grievances to his colleagues. The students agreed.

At 6:00 p.m., fifteen black students returned to Otudeko's office and gave him a letter that expressed their complaints. The letter is known as the "Initial Demands." The document expressed the students' criticisms toward the professors, claiming that they were ill-prepared to teach the course in an objective way. The professors were unqualified, they charged. The "Initial Demands" alleged that the professors depended on the black students to present to the white students their experiences living in the United States. These shared experiences were to generate discussions between the white and black students. On top of this, the professors failed to present enough material that benefited the learning experience of the black students. That failure created a one-way street, and led the students to believe they had been exploited all semester long.[34]

The "Initial Demands" document stated, "The ridiculous assumption that the black students at F&M shall be tested upon their blackness by whites is another attempt by the whiteman [sic] to assert his control over the black mentality." Arguing further, it read, "We shall not submit to the mental enslavement that whites have continually attempted to perpetrate; that enslavement in which the 'master' now 'bodaciously' [sic] attempts to tell us 'how' blacks are to think." The document set forth three demands: (1) "an apology for the exploitation of our blackness"; (2) "exemption from the final examination"; and (3) "an 'A' for every black person in Interdepartmental-4."[35] The black students felt that their role in the class was "more of a teacher than student because they spent so much of their class time describing their own experiences." The students felt that they were "guinea pigs" for the professors. One student complained to a local journalist the next day, saying that everyone "felt like rats being studied."

Professor Otudeko was able to contact five of his colleagues and tell them about the developing dilemma. (Professor Donald Tyrrell was unreachable, and Professor Murli Sinha was out of town.) He suggested that his colleagues come to his office and meet with the black students to resolve the matter that evening.

Working late on campus, the six professors discussed the "Initial Demands" and the threat concerning the final exam. According to investigative reports, they agreed that the students "had not done the reading and were scared they would flunk the course." Otudeko proposed to his colleagues that they stand firm and make the students take the final. Not one of the professors suggested talking the demands over with the black students to get to the bottom of the problem. "We reached a decision with no consultation or discussion with the students," confessed Professor Enscoe. It was "a decision which seemed extremely fair to all of us, to allow any student who wished to withdraw to do so at this point without penalty."[36] Despite the trend of student protests and sit-ins at other colleges and universities throughout the country that spring, the professors failed to see that there was a principle at stake that was more important than a grade for the African American students.

After 11:00 p.m., Otudeko telephoned Lew Thrash and invited the students back to his office so he could explain the professors' decision. Eighteen black students arrived to hear the response. The distinguished government professor Sidney Wise, who maintained a positive rapport with the college's black students, volunteered to give the report to the students. He told them that the professors were regretful for using the students like classroom props during the semester. He said "that exploitation had not been their intent and that they regretted any perception by black students which had lent itself to that interpretation." To the chagrin of the students, Wise, speaking like a lawyer, explained that there would be no automatic As, saying that if the students chose not to withdraw from the course, they would have to take the final exam.[37] He did say that he and his colleagues "would support any student petition to the Academic Standards Committee for permission to withdraw from the course."[38]

After listening to the response, the black students took a poll. What the professors were suggesting, Lew Thrash charged, was, "Now that the course is finished, now that you've helped us educate our white colleagues, now that you've filled your role as 'resource personell [*sic*],' and 'experts' in the Black Experience, you will sit down and take the same exam as the whites, and be evaluated in exactly the same terms as those whose education you have contributed to."[39] They turned to Wise, Otudeko, and the others and said with indignation that the proposal was "not acceptable."

Standing in the corner of Otudeko's office was Professor Leon Galis. Flummoxed by the students' verbal sparring, Galis thought to himself that his friend Otudeko was "in over his head." In an understandable way, he felt sorry for his colleague. Otudeko was from Nigeria, and "for all he understood about what was going on," said Galis a time later, "the black students might as well have been from another planet."[40] So Galis hovered over his colleague's shoulder as the students went on with their grievances.

Enscoe spoke up in an attempt to temper the situation. "I tried to explain that they were not being judged upon their 'blackness' but upon their reading." A student quipped back, "Then it's just a reading quiz; what's the point of that?" Not one of the professors justified their decision or proved that they understood the real problem. They still felt the grievance was over grades.

The situation grew uglier when the students began yelling. Professors Tom Glenn and Lou Athey tried to reopen the discussion with the students. But the other professors refused, saying aloud, "The matter [is] closed." As a result, the black students stormed out of the office. Steve Jacobs, a thin, five-foot-seven sophomore who typically wore African dashiki shirts and mimicked the appearance and expressions of Malcolm X, looked back at Professor Galis and threatened, "Tomorrow you will see what we will do."[41]

Galis felt slighted because Jacobs had singled him out. The professor chased after him and asked him to step aside to talk privately. He remembers, "We sat down on the steps and he began to try to explain why the black students were upset." Jacobs muttered that it had to do with "their self-respect."[42] But before he got into great detail, two of Jacobs's friends insisted he cut the conversation off and go back to Afro Hall.

Here, the professors made a critical mistake. For a reason that was never explained, they failed to report the incident to Franklin and Marshall's administration. Were they merely trying to protect the students from academic reprimand? Were they protecting themselves from an administrative investigation? Or did they not see this as an explosive issue? In any case, no matter the reason, the professors agreed to reconvene between 8:30 and 8:45 in the morning at Old Main, where they were to administer the final exam. The test was scheduled for 9:00 a.m.

When Lew Thrash and his partners returned to Afro Hall after midnight, the activity and planning shifted specifically from the students enrolled in Interdepartmental-4 to the jurisdiction of the Afro-American Society. The Society decided that they would not only boycott the exam but also ensure that no one would take the test. The strategy was to form a phalanx in front of Old Main in order to prevent the white students and the course's professors from entering the building. They believed that the blockade would be a stronger statement than simply boycotting the test by not showing up.

If anyone was still somewhat confused about the grievances of the black student community, by morning they had been firmed up. Lew Thrash and some others worked through the night penning together a document that explained their accusations against the college. They called it the "Midnight Document." At dawn they would have it photocopied and circulated around campus.[43]

Chapter 9
THE UPRISING

<hr>

A FTER STAYING UP late to create a plan that would best demonstrate the concerns of the Afro-American Society, and to best take a stand against the legacy of racism at the college, a fiery pack of students awoke early on the morning of Thursday, May 22, 1969, to begin their protest. Lancaster's two local newspapers and the investigative committee report of the incident indicated that nearly fifteen of Franklin and Marshall's fifty-eight African American students arrived early to cordon off the entrance to Old Main. A dozen white members of Students for a Democratic Society showed up in support. By 8:30 a.m. there were desks and chairs already piled in front of the doorway while all of the protesters sat or stood on the steps in front of the building waiting for the professors to arrive.[1]

After arriving together, the seven professors paused on the sidewalk in front of the building once they spotted the barricade (Murli Sinha was still out of town). Acting quickly, they conjured up a practical solution. Otudeko told the students that the exam was now a take-home test. He instructed those who had arrived early to follow him to his office inside Goethean Hall, located next to Old Main, to retrieve a test booklet, with instructions to return the exam within twenty-four hours. Meanwhile, another professor tried to post a sign outside Old Main to announce the modification to the final exam.

Henry Farrington, a white sophomore enrolled in the course, arrived late to find a crowd of black students outside both Old Main and Goethean Hall. He stood frozen as he watched the verbal exchanges between demonstrators and professors. Suddenly, a camera-wielding Benjamin Bowser walked up to him. The two college students had never spoken to one another until this moment. Bowser, who was not part of the leadership of the uprising but who had arrived that morning hoping to document history in the making, leaned in to him and said, "If you understand this [demonstration,] you understand the black experience and should pass the course. This is the test." Farrington pondered, thinking there was truth in that statement. "I look upon the incident as an expression of frustration and repression that the black race has suffered in the United States," he conceded. "It was more an expression against society than [against] F. and M."[2]

At about 8:45 a.m., all seven professors walked into Goethean Hall, moving beyond the doors leading to Otudeko's office. As Farrington and several white students followed after the professors, the demonstrators turned aggressively to their peers and used threats to dissuade them from retrieving the test.[3] The verbal sparring continued as dozens of students, black and white, entered Goethean Hall. Otudeko's office was too small to hold everyone, so the professors assembled in the seminar room across the hallway to distribute the exam. At this point, the black students forced their white peers out of the building and then blocked the front and rear exits.

The protestors, fearless and dead serious, possessed an aura of solidarity up to this point. Certainly, the blockade at Old Main and the boycott of the final exam were premeditated actions. "We had a meeting about this," remembers Afro-American Society secretary Harold Dunbar, who was not part of the disturbance. "We all agreed [the night before] that they would in a nonviolent way approach the administration about not doing well at the grades."[4] Not long after the initial standoff in front of Old Main, however, the students' actions took an unpredictable turn once they entered Goethean Hall and trapped the seven professors inside. One of those caged in was psychology professor Donald Tyrrell, who called their actions "pure spontaneous bullshit. It was totally impromptu, totally disorganized."[5]

The situation inside Goethean Hall quickly spun out of control. Reports indicate that by 9:00 a.m. the number of black demonstrators had grown to thirty, with two dozen others lingering as onlookers. Many occupied the area inside and behind Goethean.[6] People were sitting on the cold floor talking with one another. Some were reading; others, standing guard. It had the appearance of chaos and confusion, but to the students it was serious. Professor F. J. Murray, who had an office inside the building, remembers, "Some black students who had been milling around the rear door of Goethean began sitting on the floor near the rear door." The group inside Goethean became noisy after "a portable radio was brought in."[7] One of the students politely walked over to Murray's office, where he had been working. The student glanced inside, nodded, and then closed the door.

In essence, the professors had entered a spontaneous sit-in. "The sit-in, at this point," explained Murray, "was of a different scale and a different intent." He suggested that the professors "came to the sit-in; the sit-in did not come to them."[8] This contention seemingly separates the events at Franklin and Marshall from the sit-ins at other colleges and universities during 1969. The students acted on impulse. Professor Murray said, "I at no time felt that the sit-in was planned. [Instead, it seemed to be] an inevitable response to the

arrival of the faculty members to an emotionally charged situation."
Yet without formal leadership, the demonstrators suddenly cordoned
off the only door leading into and out of the seminar room by piling
chairs on either side of the door, further fencing in the professors.
Chairs were stacked in front of the door, fiberboard was packed high,
and a Gallery Upstairs sign was taken from the front entryway and
used in the barricade. Outside, student sentinels were stationed at
the front and back doors of the building, and at every window at
ground level. Many of them carried walkie-talkies. It was not until
after the barricade had been constructed that the students enforced
the ground rule that the professors could not exit the building until
their demands were met.[9]

At first, the response was disorderly as the hallway and seminar
room in Goethean Hall became congested and the professors struggled
to make sense of their incarceration. One of the boycotters named
Buck Jones moved around the building with a chair leg, suggesting it
was a stick that could be used as a weapon.[10] Professor Galis thought
it might not be a chair leg, as it had a longer appearance, much like a
broomstick. In any event, Galis remembered Jones "parading up and
down the hall outside the room and around the building brandishing
a stick about the size of a broomstick, minus the broom."[11]

One witness said fifteen black students sat or stood in the hallway,
making it uncomfortable for the other professors who had offices
inside the building. Max Drake, an anthropology professor, and
William Aho, a visiting candidate who was interviewing for a position
in the Sociology Department, were trapped inside. Drake, not taking
the demonstration seriously, casually asked the students to clear some
space in the hallway so the two of them could pass. Genially, Drake
said he "was just too old and too fat to climb through the window."[12]

The uprising increasingly turned into a tense and confusing

situation. Early on in the chain of events, a white man with a press camera entered the building. He took one picture before he was chased out and threatened. One professor whose office was in Goethean Hall, Dick Preston, received a phone call for Professor Sidney Wise, who was detained in the seminar room. Preston stepped over the barricade, moved beyond most of the students, opened the door, and inquired if Wise could take the call. "He told me that he would call them back later," remembered Preston. When Preston returned to his office, one of the black students cried out to the group of students who guarded the barrier but had let Preston through, "After this, no one crosses the barricade!"[13]

Outside of Goethean Hall there were several occasions when white students who had already received a blue book with test questions were approached by black demonstrators and forced to turn over the test. Alan Eisen, a sophomore, was able to slip by the crowd of demonstrators with a test. He took it to the library, twenty feet away from Goethean Hall, where he sat down at a table among the library's second-floor stacks to take the test. He remembers being ten minutes into the exam when a black student named Jim Craighead confronted him. Craighead, a sophomore enrolled in the Interdepartmental-4 class, reminded Eisen that there was a boycott taking place. He took Eisen's test and tore it into pieces. "I chose not to resist him," Eisen admitted. "I felt that would only add to the trouble and also cause myself personal injury." Shaken by what had just occurred, Eisen walked out to the lawn and noticed more students standing around. He said there were "exams littering the area around Goethean and Old Main."[14]

Mitchell Brecher, a junior, was also threatened by one of the boycotters. He remembers that as he left Otudeko's office with a copy of the test, "I was approached by a black student who asked me if I possessed a copy of the exam." Brecher replied that he did. "I surrendered to him the exam, whereupon he proceeded to tear it to pieces, and throw it on the ground."[15]

When Richard Rementer, a junior, arrived on campus that morning, he noticed an intimidating mass of people standing on the lawn in front of Old Main and Goethean Hall. He remembers, "I walked past them to get an examination copy and they told me, 'The examination for Interdepartmental Four has been cancelled.'" However, he said, he was able to pick up a test before the professors were barricaded inside Goethean's seminar room. After Rementer exited Goethean Hall through the back door, three protesters approached him. One asked, "Will you give up your exam peacefully, or do you want to start a ruckus?" Rementer surrendered the test and left for his dorm room with a friend who had slipped away with a blue book. "He had a copy, and I worked from that," said Rementer. "I turned it in through interdepartmental mail" before lunchtime.[16]

The uprising ruined one student's perspective on race relations. Brett Harwood was a proud sophomore at Franklin and Marshall. He said, "5 or 6 black students" surrounded him behind Goethean Hall and demanded he hand over the test. He had spent two weeks before the final exam date preparing. Harwood explained, "For many of the students in the course including myself a great deal of time was spent in research and evaluation of the questions during that two week period." He took a firm stand by refusing to forfeit the test. So the boycotters grabbed the test, gave him a little shove, and ripped it up in front of him. Harwood later wrote the college about his experience, criticizing the demonstrators. "I am Jewish and take a course in the Old Test[a]ment and the Jewish Ethics," he said. "Just because that is my religion it will be taken for granted that I know it all and will demand an 'A' in the course." He suggested in his letter to the college that the boycotters launched the uprising because they had not prepared for the final. "Perhaps many of the black students realized how much time [was] needed to be spent preparing only a short time before the exam; and not taking the exam was the only way to solve their problem."[17]

North of the quad in front of Old Main, two protestors crept ahead making their way to the college's post office, where they believed exams were going to be placed in students' mailboxes. They did not find exam blue books, but on their way out of the post office they spotted Lois Huth, Otudeko's secretary at the Anthropology Department, heading in their direction. The students recognized her, realizing she worked with Professor Otudeko. They stopped her after noticing the interoffice envelope that she was holding across her chest and demanded to know its contents. Huth admitted that she did not know. One student stepped forward and insisted, "Let me see it!" Her envelope was taken and rummaged through. The students expected to find examination papers. Instead, Huth was carrying a memorandum from anthropology professor F. J. Murray intended for the college's dean. After looking inside the envelope, the student raised his eyes and grumbled, "Okay." He then returned the envelope and allowed Huth to pass.[18]

Back inside Goethean Hall's seminar room, the dispute between the professors and students was heated. One student accused Professor Enscoe of shamefully taking advantage of his students. Enscoe responded, "The course was not a black studies program!"[19] Even later that day, Enscoe mistakenly expressed to friends that "it was designed primarily for white students," adding that black students were "welcomed, even invited, to take the course because the faculty felt their contribution would be 'invaluable' in informing the whites about black experiences." His comments reflected the confusion over the initial design of the course.

More than an hour had gone by and it was still unclear to the faculty at large what was going on at Old Main and Goethean Hall, and why a disturbance was taking place. Before 10:00 a.m., Assistant Dean of Students James Gordon was called to the office of Franklin and Marshall's president, Keith Spalding, who informed him that there was a sit-in taking place by black students at Old Main. President Spalding asked Gordon to "see what was going on." On the way Gordon saw no indication of anything out of the ordinary taking place outside of Old Main. He was unaware that seven of the college's professors were being held under duress inside Goethean Hall. When Gordon arrived at Old Main, he encountered a meeting of students of the Afro-American Society. "I knocked on the door, and asked if I might speak to Lew Thrash," explained Gordon. "I was informed that a[n Afro American] Society meeting was taking place, and that he was not available at the time." Gordon, a bit perplexed at the moment, waited in the hall until the meeting was over. As the members of the Afro-American Society were leaving Old Main, Gordon approached Thrash and asked him what was going on. Gordon said, "He was reluctant to talk to me, but did give me a copy of the three demands which were being made of the professors teaching Interdepartmental-4." At the moment, Gordon was unaware of what had taken place the night before. He looked up from the memo and asked where he could find Professor Otudeko. Thrash then told Gordon that the professors of the course were being detained inside Goethean Hall. "My first impression was that this was an orderly 'sit-in,'" confessed Gordon, "a peaceful protest with no implications of force or duress." He knew now that the situation was more serious than he had first suspected. Thrash escorted Gordon inside Goethean Hall to act as a negotiator between the students and the professors.

At this moment it becomes difficult to identify how much unanimity there was among the black students in the course and those in the Afro-American Society in terms of incarcerating the professors. Lew Myers, who was not on campus that day, believes that the others who got involved outside Old Main and Goethean Hall on May 22 did so in response to circumstances that Franklin and Marshall College had created. He said, "I tend to think that what happened with regards to this course was that instead of the black students being coerced by the black students they were coerced by the college community at large." With that, many members of the Afro-American Society impulsively got wrapped up in the uprising. Myers had graduated from Franklin and Marshall the previous year but remained on campus as an employee of the Office of Special Projects. His position of employment kept him abreast of campus events, including those of the Afro-American Society.

Myers explained that the Afro-American Society is a peculiar group. "A lot of people are in it because [they] have no other place to go." In a college with sixty African Americans out of almost two thousand total students, every black person was a member of the society. Of that number, upwards of twenty members were actually involved in the planning, functions, and work of the society. He contended, in cases like the May 22 uprising, "even [fewer]" are involved. Events like the boycott left F&M's black students in a catch-22. He suggested, "If you didn't participate in the incident you would have been damned by the black students and you would probably have been damned by the college community at large anyhow because they wouldn't know who participated and who didn't. So I think that's something that happens with regards to minority groups whether you participate or not. You're damned so you might as well participate."[20]

Many of the students were boxed in because of those circumstances. Arguably, since 1969 was the year of campus unrest, building seizures at other colleges and universities had some, if not a great, influence on Franklin and Marshall's May 22 uprising. From January up to the day of the boycott in May of that year, the universities of Minnesota, Louisville, Stanford, Brandeis, Swarthmore, Cornell, Rutgers–Newark, Duke, San Francisco State, Pittsburgh, Tennessee, and Fisk experienced their own cases of black students taking over administration halls and common areas while demanding black studies programs. Lew Myers testified to an investigation committee, "I think it was a cause for unity ... here's a chance to do something before the year's over." It seemed like a good explanation for trying to rationalize why the boycott spiraled out of control. "When you're a college student and go home for vacation one of the things I'm sure that is talked about is, 'we sat in on so and so, who'd you sit in on.' When you say you didn't sit in on somebody that's the same as when you're on the corner you're talking about this or that, one-better-type-story kind of thing."[21]

Presumably not every student of color at Franklin and Marshall was involved in the uprising, but the black student community was in a vacuum. LeRoy Pernell acknowledged, "With the exception of half a dozen folks or so, every black student [on campus] was aware and surely supportive of the issues or position that we were taking."[22] By 10:00 a.m., Gordon was being introduced to Franklin and Marshall's version of 1969 unrest.

As Gordon walked into Goethean Hall, his calm notion about the situation vacillated, as the scene inside the seminar room was puzzling. One witness described the actions of the black students as "frightened and nervous, but at the same time hostile and unyielding." One captor said he and his partners were "fully prepared to be expelled from school rather than compromise their demands." Another witness called them "confused" but loaded with "tough talk." Meanwhile, the professors were described to be "tense" and "uncertain." One of the professors said he felt "at sea, having to act in uncharted territory in what I felt was the virtually total absence of useful precedents."[23]

Inside the seminar room, Gordon found the seven Interdepartmental-4 professors sitting calmly in a circle. "The professors were discussing the idea of mailing exams home to students and giving them adequate time to mail them back for a final grade," he described. Gordon suggested to the professors that it was a bad idea. "This response would not be viewed by black students as a very satisfactory response to their demands." He added that the professors should invite the black students into their deliberations. The professors consented, but the black students in the room did not agree to participate in the brainstorming. One of the professors then suggested that they apologize just as the students wished, and then offer to give the students a "Pass/No Pass" grade for the course based on how they performed on the course's required term paper. The students said no to "Pass/No Pass." They demanded a grade of A. Gordon indicated that in either case, Pass/No Pass or even an A would have to be approved by the Committee on Academic Standing, but it would be impossible to gather the committee on short notice. So word was ushered out to gather the committee together at Goethean Hall.[24]

At this time, 11:00 a.m., Gordon had been inside Goethean Hall for over an hour. It was clear to the hostages by then that the students were a bit disorganized. But the captors did wish to maximize the professors' discomfort, especially when lunchtime brought about an unforeseen problem: nature was calling. The students debated about how to escort the faculty members to the restroom. Someone suggested that the professors should use the wastebasket as a urinal, while others suggested they hold it in. One student shared his disdain for the professors, asserting they had "PhD's and should be able to hold their water—shame on 'em!"[25] The students decided to escort professors to the restroom one at a time.

Just as a few of the professors were led to the bathroom, Benjamin Bowser with a single-lens reflex camera was going from window to window taking pictures of them inside the seminar room. It was at this instant that Professor Galis determined that the students were not staging a boycott and sit-in out of any deep sense of transgression. Albeit to himself, he reasoned that the students were "making their bones" and "collecting trophies to display on whatever networks of black activ[ism] they were part of."[26]

While Assistant Dean Gordon waited for his colleagues to return from the men's room, a black student outside of Goethean Hall handed papers through the window to one of his friends, who passed the small packet to Gordon. This document was the three-page manifesto entitled "Midnight Document." It had been widely circulated around campus earlier that morning, but it did not reach the seven faculty members until this moment.[27] It was a dramatic manifesto calling the professors "grossly unable to lend anything to the course other than their technological competency in their respective specialty." The "Midnight Document" testified that the black students led the class. It proclaimed, "We were the ones who gave inspiration to the course, we were the ones that taught whites what it was really like to be oppressed, and how such a process of oppression also destroyed the oppressor." It attacked white privilege: "We were the brothers who gave the white students and the white professors vast insights into the black psyche, the black experience, and black thought. None of this was done by either the white professors, or the white students[; without us] none of this could have been done successfully."[28]

Not a single conciliatory line was found in the text of the "Midnight Document". It possessed a daring tone, charging the professors with incompetence and exploitation. Each accusation was sandwiched by rat metaphors. One statement was that the professors "requested the black students to get up and serve as resource material ... 'please be a rat for our study of rat behavior.'" Later in the text, the authors alleged, "You misrepresent the course, use us as rats for your study of rat behavior, then throw us back with the field-mice." The words represented a historical case of distrust. "We now say to the faculty of that course, to the faculty, to the administration, to the student body of this institution, This is the rat speaking, and all you motherfuckers can go to hell! We shall receive our demands."[29]

The "Midnight Document" was quite influential in the final decision arrived at by the professors. After a few moments of agreement and disagreement, the group of professors decided to allow the students to grade themselves. Professor Enscoe explained that he "had been involved in courses in which he had assigned grades based on the student's own evaluation of his work." Gordon agreed, saying that he, too, had participated in undergraduate classes where he had been asked to evaluate himself. Gordon indicated, "In response to the fear that students would give themselves an A at all times, [I mentioned] that I did not give myself an A in that situation."[30] It was a negotiated peace, but the professors had struggled to find the best possible solution.

As the professors were devising a proposal, and as the quandary approached its fourth hour, Harold Dunbar, a senior on the verge of entering the University of Virginia Law School who shared a deep bond with Professor Sidney Wise, arrived on the scene to reason with his peers. Dunbar had been at the geology lab studying for his science final when a friend ran into the room and said, "Your dad called for you." Dunbar recalled, "My dad said he was watching television and he saw that the students had taken over Old Main." His father, Ulysses, who had worked two jobs in Harrisburg, Pennsylvania, to send Harold and his sister, Paula, to college, reminded him, "We had a deal. You're going to graduate in four years and you're going to stay away from trouble." Dunbar replied, "I don't know anything about that, [D]ad, [but] I'm going to look into it." When Dunbar arrived at Goethean Hall, he saw a bunch of his friends walking around "with sticks and bats." He spent the next hour helping to diffuse the situation. Dunbar walked into Goethean Hall and said, "Come on now, what do you plan to do, cut them?"[31] After conveying to his friends the seriousness of the recent January student uprising at Swarthmore College, which resulted in the death of the college's president, Courtney C. Smith, and the April armed takeover at Cornell University, he "reminded the guys that the national guard would likely be called in."[32]

As Dunbar tried to reason with his peers, the Committee on Academic Standing finally arrived at Goethean Hall and was informed about the proposal that was discussed. The committee members explained that if the self-grading proposal was the final decision, they would not need to approve it. Then, with the committee in the room, the seven professors secretly voted on the proposal to allow the students to choose their own grade for the course.

Not every professor was in favor of the self-grading proposal. Professor Galis asked his colleagues if there was "something like a policy of 'any arguments made under duress are null and void.'" His inquiry prompted a nasty conversation about how the college might react. According to the investigative report of the incident, four of the seven members of the Committee on Academic Standing "found the self-grading proposal unobjectionable to varying degrees and on various grounds." Likewise, Assistant Dean Gordon found the proposal unobjectionable. Professor Sidney Wise turned to Professor Enscoe, who stood out as the proposal's biggest proponent, and asked if he was urging the adoption of the proposal "just to get out of the room."[33] Enscoe defended his support, claiming it was the best possible solution.

When the professors finally voted among themselves on the option of letting the students self-grade, the proposal passed 4 to 3. Otudeko, Enscoe, Tom Glenn, and a reluctant Leon Galis voted in favor,* with Louis Athey, Sidney Wise, and Donald Tyrrell voting against allowing students to grade themselves.[34]

Professor Otudeko informed the black students of the decision. He expressed his sympathies for those who felt exploited, and added, "There had been no intent on [the professors'] part to exploit anyone." He told the students that they would be able to evaluate their performance based on "at least a term paper." Otudeko also said that the final exam was now optional.

Without a conference, the black students looked at one another and nodded. "Yeah, we'll take it." In hindsight, it was a hasty reaction after a long morning. After the students audaciously spent the morning demanding an A grade, suddenly there "was just a nodding of heads, a look," and acceptance of the professors' offer, Lew Myers said critically. There was "no, 'let us take five minutes to see if this is what we want.'"[35] But now that it was done, it was too late to recant.

---

* Leon Galis changed his vote after the fact when the college staff at large renegotiated the consequences of the May 22 uprising.

LeRoy Pernell dismisses their decision as an injudicious settlement, instead believing that they made their point. "I think the issues of recognition, of understanding the importance of an African American voice and perspective" were at the heart of the uprising. "I think that those points were made," Pernell noted. "If you're familiar with Ralph Ellison's work, [you'll understand that] we were no longer the invisible man."[36]

Before the boycott came to its conclusion, the black students insisted on a written apology and a promise that there would not be disciplinary action taken against anyone involved in the uprising. Gordon said, "It seemed like insult was being added to injury."[37] Nonetheless, the professors agreed. The professors gave assurances that they would not press charges against the students, but they cautioned that could not prevent the college from taking disciplinary action against them.

Everyone waited patiently as Professor Otudeko wrote his apology. During that time Gordon turned to the black students and told them that he was proud of the way the professors had handled the situation. "I felt that the seven professors had worked toward a solution despite the fact that there was unnecessary pressure upon them to arrive at a solution," he said. Once he had completed it, Otudeko read the written apology.

At 1:15 p.m., the students accepted the results and the faculty were permitted to leave the building. Before their departure from Goethean Hall, each of the professors pledged to one another that they would avoid speaking with the members of the media who were waiting outside for their release. All but one of the professors kept his word. Remarks made by Professor Enscoe appeared in a newspaper the following day. "We all agreed in that room that we would not talk to the press," said an annoyed Professor Tyrrell. "[Enscoe] was talking to reporters as I walked out."[38]

Minutes after their release, most of the professors had returned to their offices. Back at his office, Professor Galis experienced a strange encounter. There, he found one of the demonstrators waiting. Galis never identified which student it was, but he was one of the demonstrators and an author of the "Initial Demands" and "Midnight Document" texts. Galis invited him into his office. The student asked Galis to grade his performance in the course. "By now," Galis admitted, "I was already in a state of confusion that had been intensifying since the night before." The request baffled him. The student was planning on submitting his "self-assigned" grade to Professor Otudeko, but he wanted reassurance from Galis, someone whom the student trusted, before he did so. Galis refused. He told the student that after what he had just experienced, it was inconceivable that he could be asked to "renounce the agreement that the black students had only just then undergone considerable risk" to squeeze from the professors.[39] The conversation was cordial; each man expressed the amount of respect he held for the other. Galis invited the student to return to his office the following day so they could continue their conversation. The student said he would return, but he did not.

At 2:00 p.m., the seven professors and Assistant Dean Gordon were talking about the incident with President Spalding.

Chapter 10
THE INVESTIGATION

A STEADY STREAM OF faculty, many in a frenzy of speculation, flowed onto campus that evening. At 5:00 p.m. the entire faculty met and listened to the Interdepartmental-4 professors express regret for both giving in to the students' demands and granting them amnesty earlier that day. "We regret the fact that these questions were not formally raised earlier in the semester," one of the professors conceded. "However, we insist that the procedures utilized today and the decisions which resulted are in no way a precedent for future deliberations on this campus."

Leon Galis spent a lot of time defending his Interdepartmental-4 colleagues. "It is worth noting, I think, that Professor Otudeko, from the beginning and throughout this affair, discounted the 'exploitation' charge as nothing more than an attempt to mask the real factors at work," he explained. Galis and his colleagues implied that the students felt "intense pressure academically," and from the conception of the "Initial Demands" to the end of the uprising, they "dreamed up the exploitation charge as a way of justifying demands that would get them off the hook academically … in a course in which they would naturally expect to do quite well."[1]

Galis also expressed his frustrations. He especially criticized his own support of the proposal to allow students the opportunity to grade themselves. "I felt intensely uneasy about [that] on academic grounds," he admitted. Galis had voted in favor of the proposal, but he contended that he was swayed by several factors. The morning of the uprising was long and tiresome. By one o'clock in the afternoon, he grew hungry and was worried about how he would let his wife know that he was fine. He thought back to the first day of class when he admitted that he needed help from the black students to relate his lecture points to the nation's contemporary issues.[2] He did not feel, however, that the comment was reason enough for the students to hold him and his colleagues under duress. Galis said years later with resentment, "Somebody may have treated them like 'resource material,' but I certainly didn't."[3]

Many in the faculty were aghast at the report. Some called for immediate action. They wanted serious retribution against the professors' captors. President Spalding said no action would be taken at that moment since the meeting had been called only to pass along information and to quash rumors that had been floating around campus. Yet, he was disturbed. In light of his colleagues' remarks, Spalding replied flatly, "[I have] deep concern with the manner in which the demands were presented and the way faculty members' efforts to reach a reasonable solution were received." Spalding said, "the faculty will meet again to discuss further the dangers to academic freedom and integrity which lie in any use of threat or coercion in communication between faculty and students."[4] Nothing else was reported that evening.

Over the course of the next three days, the college administration depended on feedback from colleagues, its student body, and community leaders. After a long weekend, the College Senate convened on Monday, May 27, at Stahr Hall for its first session since the May 22 uprising. The senate was made up of fifteen faculty members and three students, all elected, plus President Spalding and Dean of Students O. W. Lacy.[5]

At the meeting, Galis offered the motion to renege on the agreement to let the Interdepartmental-4 students grade themselves. He claimed that the vote had been taken under duress. "Since I didn't think that what we agreed to in order to get out of the room without anybody getting hurt or being charged with a criminal offense was even remotely like the Japanese surrender aboard the USS *Missouri*, I had no compunction what[so]ever about introducing the motion ... declaring the agreement null and void," Galis pronounced years later.[6] The College Senate vote was not binding, but it was sent to the entire faculty for a discussion and subsequent vote. The college faculty passed the measure.

Nearly simultaneously, President Spalding issued a six-page statement that was ultimately printed in Lancaster's *Intelligencer Journal*. In it, he told the community, "Violent disruption or forcible interference with the orderly activity at Franklin and Marshall is intolerable." Spalding's statement was a valid effort to maintain personal control. His attempt on the offensive illustrated Franklin and Marshall College as a tolerant institution that had long worked to prevent eruptions like what happened on May 22, 1969. "The problem of campus unrest is more than a campus problem," he contended. "Its roots lie deep in the larger society. There is no single cause, no single solution." He called Franklin and Marshall "second to none among colleges and universities." He defended the college's commitment to multicultural credence and its brand of collegiality.

> In the events of May 21–22, we have suddenly learned much about the rolling distress and disorder which follow a circumvention of the orderly academic process ... We learned how quickly the academic

process becomes the victim when the mere suggestion of physical restraint or intimidation is brought into play. We learn how suddenly the college community is offended when one group is perceived as seeking special privilege or as limiting the rights of others.[7]

Despite President Spalding's attempts to validate his college's academic integrity, it did not take long until Franklin and Marshall heard the outcry from the community on the editorial pages of the two local newspapers: the *Intelligencer Journal* and the *Lancaster New Era*. Written by someone using the pseudonym Mildly Upset: '64 F&M Grad, one editorial read, "I am particularly concerned with the demand for an 'A' grade for all of the black students ... I do not feel that an institution which commands the respect that Franklin and Marshall College does has to subject itself to any of this academic 'blackmail' perpetrated by an ever increasing number of 'I-demand' rather than 'I'll work for' students." The letter's author pressed, "To give credence to these demands and this demand in particular can only lead to more of these absurd decrees, and eventually the state of anarchy which exists on many of the larger campuses."[8] The last assertion made clear reference to similar episodes that had occurred across the country at universities like Rutgers, Swarthmore, Cornell, and Duke, where student takeovers and armed building seizures had also occurred in 1969. In each case, administrations capitulated to students' demands and took limited or no legal action.

Another letter to the editor bristled with criticism: "Why did the faculty, voting as a whole [after the hostage standoff,] support the actions of the [seven] terrified professors?" The writer, using the pseudonym Concerned Alumnus, went on, "Yesterday we were treated to a lengthy newspaper statement by President Spalding claiming F&M won't 'tolerate violent disruption,' and adding 'students could be expelled.' Words, words, words! Is not holding seven professors hostage for five hours 'violent disruption'?" The harsh words persisted. "The local college must be mighty proud to be in the same league with Columbia, Cornell ... institutions administered by faculty and or presidents who do not have backbones."[9]

The criticism of both the administration and the black students who were enrolled in the Interdisciplinary-4 course did not end in the columns of the local newspapers. Twenty-four hours after the incident, letters from Franklin and Marshall students began appearing at the dean's office. Jack Flom condemned the actions of the college's black students who took part in the sit-in. "Common law principle has for generations maintained that a contract signed at knife-point is null and void. While this decision was not exactly reached at knife-point, there was certainly enough duress exercised to prohibit rational discourse before a decision was made." Flom contended that the black students were supposed to be graded on their proven understanding of the information they received from the course, not on what they had added to the course. "There is also the very practical and legalistic argument that any student who signed up for the course obligated himself to fulfill the obligations listed in the syllabus, withdraw, or pay the consequences," Flom added before he made one final remark. "I would recommend that the aforementioned decision be reversed, and that the students should not be allowed to grade themselves."[10]

Out of view, and notwithstanding the public's brooding, the administrative team did a fine job in damage-control mode, going into overdrive to clean up the image of their college. Their efforts to find quick solutions were remarkable. The college overruled the agreement made between the seven faculty members that the black students may assign themselves grades in the course. President Spalding said, "The agreement was reached under duress, since the seven faculty members were told by black students that they could not leave the room in which they were meeting until they reached conclusions satisfactory to the students." Spalding admitted that he was "surprised" at the actions of the students. He said, "Previous contacts with groups of black students and with the leaders of the Afro-American Society have resulted in candid, searching discussions." He added, "This was the first time that any group of students had resorted to threat of force."[11] The college's faculty overwhelmingly supported the decision. Notably, it became the first time in a weary year of campus disruptions nationally that a college had reversed a decision made during a racial confrontation.

There was one major crisis, however. It was May 28, and most of the students had already departed for summer break. Just 25 percent of the student body remained on campus, most of them seniors waiting for graduation. Two of Franklin and Marshall's seniors were black students enrolled in the Interdepartmental-4 course. The professors of the course, adhering to the decision made by both the College Senate and the Committee on Professional Standards, came up with a solution for how to grade their pupils. It was determined that seniors would be given credit for completing the course, but no grade.[12] This would make the two African American seniors eligible to graduate.

Underclassmen were approached differently, however. The Committee on Professional Standards and the college faculty reported that each student in the Interdepartmental-4 course already had a grade based on his term paper and class participation. Each student was then given two options if he was unhappy with his grade: either writing a final exam, the grade of which would be averaged with the term paper and class participation grades, or electing for a "Pass/No Pass" grade.[13]

President Spalding subsequently announced that the college was continuing its investigation into the hostage incident at Goethean Hall and the circumstances surrounding the conception of the course. "An event of this sort," Spalding rationalized, "is an infinitely complex matter. It requires the most intensive investigation to know the causes of the sudden action of the students which seemed to develop through events improvised on the spot rather than through a pre-arranged plan." He pledged to get to the bottom of the incident, "as well as to assess the culpability of the persons who were involved."[14] Spalding announced that an ad hoc committee made up of young community leaders from Lancaster City, secondary educators, and professors from Franklin and Marshall's faculty would continue the inquiry of the incident.

The Western Committee, named after its chairman Donald Western, a distinguished mathematics professor, had permission to use staff and budgetary services at the college. It was allowed to seek relevant information from any source either on or off the campus that would help acquire specific details related to the case. Western's "blue ribbon" committee, as President Spalding called it, made it clear that its purpose was not responsible for gathering evidence to discipline any individual.[15] Its sole purpose was to find out the root causes of events like the May 22 uprising and to discern how the college could avoid future instances.*

---

* The ad hoc committee's chairman was Professor Donald Western, the chair of the Mathematics Department at Franklin and Marshall College. Also serving on the committee were John Joseph, a professor of history and an alumnus of the college; Toby Roberts Appel, an attorney and an alumnus of Franklin and Marshall; Ronald Potier, admissions director at Franklin and Marshall; John Schropshire, a high school teacher in the Harrisburg School District and member of the PREP staff at Franklin and Marshall; and two students, Gregg Colvin and Buddy Glover, from Franklin and Marshall and Gettysburg College respectively. Colvin, '72, was a member of the student government at F&M. Glover, '71, was a Seventh Ward native and a history major at Gettysburg. Glover was well known at F&M, mostly because of his enrollment in the 1967 PREP program. His brother Darryl, mentioned in chapter 5, led the liberation walkout of McCaskey High School the day after Martin Luther King's assassination.

After a six-month investigation, the Western Committee outlined a range of complex problems at Franklin and Marshall. In late November 1969, almost a full semester after the disturbance, the committee's publication reminded everyone at Franklin and Marshall just how fragile the campus environment really was. It recognized the "sincere good intentions" and "substantial efforts" of the eight professors who had invented and volunteered to teach the class. The committee called the course an "experiment" that was a "valid effort" to reach out to the college's students of color. The course, however, according to the committee, fell greatly short of its objective.

The details in the Western Committee's final report were as clear as possible. The committee criticized Otudeko and his colleagues for their inability to effectively communicate their expectations to the students. Drawing out the obvious implications from the semester's curious chain of events, the report noted, "Confusion developed as to whether the course was the first step toward a full program of Black studies, as the students said they were led to believe, or was simply an experimental effort by a group of concerned faculty to introduce a course dealing with black thought in America."[16] By midsemester, the black students in the class grew apprehensive. They started to shut down. The dynamic between students and professors shifted over the term of the course. The students were more skeptical of the professors; the professors became even more assertive. The estrangement caused students to ignore details about the term paper, which resulted in poor grades. This did not help the relationship, which spiraled even more out of control when the study guide for the final examination was distributed to the students.

This was not the only mistake that the Western Committee identified. It also criticized the professors for failing to communicate with the college's administration immediately after Lew Thrash and others threatened to boycott the final on the evening of May 21. The report contended that the May 22 uprising could have been avoided.

Problematic as the professors' negligence was, the Western Committee was more critical of the black students. The committee found the students' decision to incarcerate the professors inside the seminar room at Goethean Hall "unacceptable." Noting the "tense and uncertain" situation, the committee praised the professors for their ability to handle the pressure of being held hostage. "The fact that a resolution was accomplished was most fortuitous for all concerned,"[17] the report applauded. It urged that none of the students be prosecuted for their actions.

The committee's youngest member, Buddy Glover, a Seventh Ward resident who was attending Gettysburg College at the time of the disturbance, authored the minority opinion, which was at variance with the Western Committee's. Glover provided a sympathetic perspective, arguing that the students' actions were explicable. Since there were just two black professors and one black administrator on campus, the college was unprepared to provide faculty capable enough to deal with the issues that were raised during the course. Glover's minority report unleashed a torrent of issues to be considered. White students at Franklin and Marshall College outnumbered black students 30 to 1. Although liberal, the white community was alien to the needs of its black students, since all of Franklin and Marshall's students of color were from urban areas. That meant a black student most likely lived in a black neighborhood, which warranted acquaintances with people of the same color. Those students from the South had almost certainly attended a predominantly black high school. Prior to arriving at Franklin and Marshall College, a black student's contact with whites was in all probability limited to a patrolman on his block. And in this case, it is likely that any encounter with someone of a different race was negative rather than positive. Yet, suddenly upon arriving on campus, a black student was thrown into an unfamiliar world. Most likely his roommate was white, that is, until a black student became an upperclassman and could request a roommate. Often, the associates of a white roommate persisted in reminding the black student that he was, in fact, a person of color. Moreover, the fact that the college failed to provide a fraternal house for its black students added to the perception that Franklin and Marshall was insensitive to the concerns of its students of color.

The dilemma was not limited to the dormitory. With a faculty of just two black professors, any student of color on campus most likely sought council from an academic adviser, professor, or dean who was white. Glover emphasized in earnest, "There are things black people just cannot freely communicate to white people, regardless of their background and qualifications." As a result, black students, whether at Franklin and Marshall or any another university, demanded both curriculum reforms and social reforms. "The educational system as it operates today continues to reinforce and perpetuate the racism which runs rampant in this society," Glover reasoned. He wrote, "Not only white students are not taught to respect black people, but black students are turned against black people." It was contended that if study of the work of African American heroes like W. E. B. Du Bois, Frederick Douglass, and Langston Hughes was absent from courses in literature, history, and sociology, then, as Glover pointed out, "one can only deduce from those circumstances that those black people were insignificant."[18]

As if extracted from the Liberty Paints Plant in Ralph Ellison's timeless novel *Invisible Man*, Glover's assertions are vital to understanding the course's structural flaws and the lack of racial empathy presented in Interdepartmental-4 at the end of the semester. Like Ellison's Optic White paint, which possessed the ability to whiten charcoal, current pedagogical practices at Franklin and Marshall, Glover contested, compelled students of color to mask their true thoughts and feelings about society so that they could blend in to white culture. Glover's first complaint was aimed at the differences in the teaching methods of each professor. Some instructors held closely to the line of objectively presenting the subject matter, whereas others depended more on interpretations arising out of student participation. The professors found it difficult to balance the class discussions with the assigned reading materials and lectures. Black students began complaining when they were assigned class presentations when none of the white students were asked or expected to do the same. The second misunderstanding was that the black students felt that the class was supposed to provide them with "personal enlightenment" about their own "blackness" in American society. The class was supposed to help them understand how racial minorities fit into American society. However, the structure and content of the class made it appear as if the black students were the resources, or laboratory rats, for white students in the class to test out their own theories.

Although the investigation had finally concluded, the feelings of those involved in the uprising, professors and students alike, were not put at ease. Still troubled by what occurred, Professor Thomas Glenn said that the Afro-American Society and the Students for a Democratic Society were unable to look "beyond their personal affairs" to see how their issues were national concerns. "The distrust" between Franklin and Marshall and those two student-led societies, Glenn added, "prevents the college from taking a stand as a [college] community or institution on any contemporary issue."

Benjamin Bowser gave a response to Glenn's assertion in the

1969 yearbook *Oriflamme* before he graduated. He said, "If Franklin and Marshall is to be described as a community of Men in pursuit of truth and its consequences in any sense of the word, then it is a wasteland." He was speaking sincerely; Bowser saw some "individual administrators who have an active concern over national problems," but said that with the exception of those few men, "F&M mirrors no concern" about the issues of the Afro-American Society or national anxieties. He acrimoniously planned to accept his diploma. "There is no relation between my personal life, which is outside of F&M, and F&M," he said. "I am a visitor from another country."[19]

How does one view the behavior of the students involved in the uprising? The portrait that emerges from a careful examination of the May 22 uprising is an image of unruly students overstepping their bounds, first by staging a boycott in front of Old Main, next by tearing up their classmates' take-home tests, and finally by holding their professors under duress. Their anger, however, was an appendage of the issues of a wounded nation: the Vietnam War, the draft with its rank-in-class question, increasingly politicized campus environments, the counterculture, chemical experimentation, the assassinations of Martin Luther King, Malcolm X, and Medgar Evers, the three previous summers of inner-city riots, the influence of an expanding Black Panther Party, and the examples set by other student takeovers on campuses across the nation. These events had affected them on a personal level, feeding the growing conviction that they were an alienated race in the United States of America.

These were teenagers and twenty-somethings with valid perspectives about the systemic racism existing within the Franklin and Marshall College environment, yet their concerns included a taste of misguided self-righteousness created by the political climate. That fact makes the effort to understand this uprising a puzzling one.

The students at Franklin and Marshall College were not criminals or thugs. They were intense, career-driven young men who could have passed the course readily if they would have treated it like any other on their schedule. What they did, however, damaged the viewpoint of many open-minded white students on campus. Additionally, a few of the professors who were detained inside Goethean Hall were emotionally scarred, left dejected that their lifelong commitment to social justice was disregarded so abruptly by their students of color.

The title of the course plays a small, but understandable, role in vindicating the students' actions. By calling the course the Black Experience in America, the professors set their own trap, which took the form of the May 22 uprising. Additionally, the course's reading list was daunting, arguably too excessive for an undergraduate course that included a term paper and a final exam. Malcontents in the class had been rallying support within the Afro-American Society during the late weeks of the semester, which is why as the end of the term approached, whatever optimism had existed was replaced by antipathy.

Perhaps a sad outcome of the events of May 22, 1969, was that Franklin and Marshall College waited until the nineties to implement a black studies interdisciplinary program. For decades, the debate once taken up between the Afro-American Society and the concerned faculty was an afterthought. But in 1992, two students collected over eight hundred signatures on a petition supporting the establishment of a black studies field. At that point in history, scholarship inevitably shifted the national academic direction toward diaspora studies. Therefore, Africana Studies, an interdisciplinary program, was approved as a minor for undergraduates on April 27, 1994. Three years later, it was incorporated as a major.[20]

Whether in 1969 or 1994, there is a very important lesson about empathy that should be learned from the May 22 uprising. Comprised within that struggle was the connection between African American students and those in the community as they worked, in a small way, to liberate their race from a society underpinned by the long systemic tradition of segregation. At the forefront of the students' struggle was the need for pedagogical change, namely, to create a black studies department. As the college delayed the creation of that program, the black community in Lancaster City filled the void. Franklin and Marshall's black students became ingrained in race liberation and black power dogma promoted in the Seventh Ward, which was the same ideology disseminated in black communities across the country. So whether on campus or off, the experiences of Franklin and Marshall's African American students have become, in an important respect, the story of all people of color grappling with the effort to shape the dialogue about race throughout the country in any era.

SOURCES

BOOKS AND MAGAZINES

Bermanzohn, Sally Avery. *Through Survivors' Eyes: From the Sixties to the Greensboro Massacre*. Nashville: Vanderbilt University Press, 2003.

Bloom, Joshua, and Waldo Martin. *Black Against Empire: The History and Politics of the Black Panther Party*. Berkeley: University of California Press, 2013.

Bryant, Drayton S. *Ongoing Neighborhood Self-Renewal: Recommendations for Housing Programs and Related Services, Church-Musser Renewal Area, Lancaster, Pa.* Philadelphia: D. S. Bryant, 1967.

Clay, Marianne. "Prepsters of the Past." *Franklin and Marshall Newsletter*, Winter 2000.

Davis, Angela Yvonne. *Angela Davis: An Autobiography*. New York: International Publishers, 1974.

Downs, Donald Alexander. *Cornell: Liberalism and the Crisis of the American University*. Ithaca: Cornell University Press, 1999.

Dyson, Michael Eric. *The Black Presidency: Barack Obama and the Politics of Race in America*. New York: Houghton Mifflin Harcourt, 2016.

Franklin and Marshall College. *Bulletin of Franklin & Marshall College*. Lancaster: Franklin and Marshall, July 1965.

———. 1965, 1966, 1967, 1968, and 1969 yearbooks entitled *Oriflamme*. Lancaster: Shadek-Fackenthal Library.

Glaude, Eddie S., Jr. *Democracy in Black: How Race Still Enslaves the American Soul*. New York: Crown/Archetype, 2016.

Hill, Marc Lamont. *Nobody: Casualties of America's War on the Vulnerable, from Ferguson to Flint and Beyond*. New York: Atria Books, 2016.

"It Can't Happen Here, Can It?" *Newsweek*. May 5, 1969, 26–30.

Joseph, Peniel E. *The Black Power Movement: Rethinking the Civil Rights–Black Power Era*. New York: Routledge, 2006.

———. *Waiting 'til the Midnight Hour: A Narrative History of Black Power in America*. New York: Henry Holt and Company, 2006.

Kibler, Alison, and Mollie Ruben. "Lancaster at Play." Lancaster: Lancaster County Historical Society, 2007.

Massaquoi, Hans J. "Fired Black Muslim denounces cult, vows to take part in rights revolt." *Ebony*. September 1964.

Newton, Huey P. *Huey Newton Speaks: Prelude to Revolution*. Interview with Huey P. Newton. By Mark Lane. 47 min. Pardon Records, 1971.

Office of Special Programs. *Prepster Yearbook*. Lancaster: Franklin and Marshall College, 1967.

Ogbar, Jeffrey O. G. *Black Power: Radical Politics and African American Identity*. Baltimore: Johns Hopkins University Press, 2005.

Schultz, Bud, and Ruth Schultz. *The Price of Dissent: Testimonies to Political Repression in America*. Berkeley: University of California Press, 2001.

Schuyler, David. *A City Transformed: Redevelopment, Race, and Suburbanization in Lancaster, Pennsylvania, 1940–1980*. University Park: Pennsylvania State University Press, 2000.

Seale, Bobby. *Seize the Time: The Story of the Black Panther Party and Huey P. Newton*. New York: Random House, 1971.

Winkler, Adam. "The Secret History of Guns." *Atlantic Magazine*. September 2011. Accessed June 16, 2015. http://www.theatlantic.com/magazine/archive/2011/09/the-secret-history-of-guns/308608/.

COURT CASES

Commonwealth v. Figari et al. 166 Pa. Super. 169 (1950). Superior Court of Pennsylvania. Argued September 27, 1949.

INTERVIEWS

Bethea, Benjamin. Personal interview by the author. Lancaster, PA. October 9, 2007.

Bowser, Benjamin P. Telephone interview by the author. Hayward, CA. July 18, 2012.

(Brown) Washington, Ramilee. Telephone interview by the author. Lancaster, PA. March 16, 2014.

Butcher, Louis. Personal interview by the author. Brightside Baptist Church, Lancaster, PA. July 27, 2012.

Craighead, James. Personal interview by the author. Harrisburg, PA. August 11, 2012.

Dunbar, Harold. Telephone interview by the author. Harrisburg, PA. October 8, 2015.

Ford, Elizabeth. Personal interview by the author. Mountville, PA. September 29, 2015.

Ford, Ronald. Personal interview by the author. Lancaster, PA. March 18, 2016.

Franklin, George. Personal interview by the author. Harrisburg, PA. August 1, 2012.

Galis, Leon. E-mail correspondence with the author. Athens, GA. February 10, 2015.

Glover, Leon ("Buddy"). Personal interview by the author. Lancaster, PA. May 7, 2013.

Hopkins, Leroy. Personal interview by the author. Millersville, PA. August 9, 2012.

(Leet) Pittenger, Pauline. Personal interview by the author. Lancaster, PA. January 14, 2014.

———. Personal interview by the author. Lancaster, PA. February 4, 2014.

(Lucas) Gillis, Shirley. Telephone interview by the author. Lancaster, PA. March 15, 2014.

Myers, Lewis H. Telephone interview by the author. Durham, NC. January 22, 2014.

———. Telephone interview by the author. Durham, NC. February 13, 2014.

Pernell, LeRoy. Telephone interview by the author. Orlando, FL. August 3, 2012.

Reed, Fred. Personal interview by the author. Harrisburg, PA. September 24, 2007.

Schaeffer, J. Donald. Personal interview by the author. Lancaster, PA. August 5, 2012.

Schuyler, David. Personal interview by the author. Olmsted Building, Franklin and Marshall College, Lancaster, PA. February 11, 2014.

Tyrrell, Donald J. Personal interview by the author. Millersville, PA. January 21, 2014.

Val-Kambourglos, Nancy. Interview by Corey Conyers. Lancaster, PA. August 14, 2007.

Wilson, Gerald. Telephone interview by the author. Lancaster, PA. September 6, 2007.

———. Telephone interview by the author. Lancaster, PA. October 7, 2007.

NEWSPAPERS

College Reporter (Franklin and Marshall College, Lancaster, PA)

Courier Times (Bucks County, PA)

Intelligencer Journal (Lancaster, PA)

Lancaster New Era (Lancaster, PA)

New York Times (New York, NY)

Spokesman Review (Spokesman, WA)

UNPUBLISHED FILES AND TRANSCRIPTS, AND VIDEOS

Ad Hoc Investigative Committee. "Ad Hoc Committee Investigative May 22." June 30, 1969. Buddy Glover Files. Lancaster, PA.

———. "Critical Analysis, First Revision." October 27, 1969. Buddy Glover Files. Lancaster, PA.

———. "Exhibit B: Interdepartmental-4: The Black Experience in America. Course Syllabus. February 4, 1969." Buddy Glover Files. Lancaster, PA.

———. "Exhibit C: Professor Otudeko, Black Experience in America Examination Questions. April 30, 1969." Buddy Glover Files. Lancaster, PA.

———. "Exhibit E. Initial Demands by the Black Students. May 21, 1969." Buddy Glover Files. Lancaster, PA.

———. "Exhibit F: Midnight Document. May 22, 1969." Buddy Glover Files. Lancaster, PA.

———. "Exhibit G: The Report of the Incident at Franklin and Marshall. May 22, 1969." Buddy Glover Files. Lancaster, PA.

———. Meeting minutes, May 22, 1969. Buddy Glover Files. Lancaster, PA.

———. "The following is a resolution passed by unanimous vote." July 1, 1969. Buddy Glover Files. Lancaster, PA.

Africana Studies Program Committee. "Proposal for the Establishment of a Major in Africana Studies." Franklin and Marshall College, Lancaster, PA. January 1999.

Franklin and Marshall College. Shadek-Fackenthal Library Archives and Special Collections Department. Political and Social Action Organizations. Afro-American Society Folder.

———. Shadek-Fackenthal Library Archives and Special Collections Department. Special Programs Box. PREP: The Pre-College Enrichment Program at F&M Folder.

Gilmore, Tom. "Afro-American Society, Prospectus." October 20, 1968. Franklin and Marshall College. Buddy Glover Files. Lancaster, PA.

Lathan, Stan. *Say Brother. Black Power on University Campuses.* Boston: WGBH, 1969. 58 mins.

Martin, Hubert R., and Robert V. Rivers. "Black People's Defense League." May, 1968. Buddy Glover Files. Lancaster, PA.

Penn, Michael L. "Proposal of the Africana Studies Program Committee Transition to a Major in Africana Studies." Franklin and Marshall College, Lancaster, PA. April 8, 1998.

Stameshkin, David M. *A History of Fraternities and Sororities at Franklin and Marshall College, 1854–1987.* Franklin and Marshall College. Shadek-Fackenthal Library Archives and Special Collections Department.

Western, Donald, et al. "Final Report of the Ad Hoc Investigative Committee." November 7, 1969. Office of Public Relations, Franklin and Marshall College, Lancaster, PA. Buddy Glover Files.

LETTERS

Afro-American Society. "Black Culture Center." January 19, 1970. Franklin and Marshall College. Shadek-Fackenthal Library Archives and Special Collections Department. Political and Social Action Organizations. Afro-American Society Folder.

Black Students of Interdepartmental-4 and the Black Students at Franklin and Marshall. "Position Paper: Black Students of Interdepartmental-Four." May 25, 1969. Buddy Glover Files. Lancaster, PA.

Brecher, Mitchell. Letter to the ad hoc investigative committee. Lancaster, PA. May 24, 1969. Buddy Glover Files. Lancaster, PA.

Eisen, Alan, et. al. "To College Senate." May 23, 1969. Buddy Glover Files. Lancaster, PA.

———. Letter to Donald Western and the ad hoc investigative committee. July 28, 1969. Buddy Glover Files. Lancaster, PA.

Enscoe, Gerald E. Letter to Donald Western and the ad hoc investigative committee. August 9, 1969. Buddy Glover Files. Lancaster, PA.

Farrington, Henry. Letter to Donald Western and the ad hoc investigative committee. ca. August 1969. Buddy Glover Files. Lancaster, PA.

Flom, Jack, et. al. Letter to the College Senate. May 1969. Buddy Glover Files. Lancaster, PA.

Gordon, James H. Letter to the ad hoc investigative committee, "Recollections of events of May 22, 1969." July 16, 1969. Buddy Glover Files. Lancaster, PA.

Harwood, Brett. Letter to Donald Western and the ad hoc investigative committee. ca. August 1969. Buddy Glover Files. Lancaster, PA.

Murray, F. J. Letter to Donald Western and the ad hoc investigative committee. October 10, 1969. Buddy Glover Files. Lancaster, PA.

Myers, Lewis H. "The Black Student at F&M, a pamphlet designed to give prospecting students an idea of how a former black F&M College student—class of '68—views his Alma Mater." Office of Special Programs, Franklin and Marshall College. Lancaster, PA. 1968.

———. "Luncheon Interview, August 18, 1969: Committee 5-22 with Lew Myers." Buddy Glover Files. Lancaster, PA.

Preston, Dick. Letter to Don Western, ad hoc investigative committee. August 1, 1969. Buddy Glover Files. Lancaster, PA.

Rementer, Richard. Letter to Dr. Donald Western and the ad hoc investigative committee. ca. July 1969. Buddy Glover Files. Lancaster, PA.

WEBSITES

Schuyler, David. *Urban Renewal and the Changing Face of Lancaster* (Franklin and Marshall College, Lancaster, PA, 2014). Accessed September 7, 2016. http://www.fandm.edu/david-schuyler/changing-face-of-lancaster.

Vollmer, Russ. "Class of 1962 History" (Franklin and Marshall College, Lancaster, PA, n.d.). Accessed September 7, 2016. fandm.edu/uploads/files/738980208707108066-class-of-1962-history.original.pdf.

Washington University Libraries. "Eyes on the Prize II Interviews." Angela Davis. Interview by Terry Rockefeller and Louis Massiah. May 24, 1989 (camera rolls 3107–11; sound Rolls: 340–50). Accessed September 7, 2016. http://digital.wustl.edu/e/eii/eiiweb/dav5427.0115.036marc_record_interviewer_process.html.

NOTES

INTRODUCTION

1 Ad Hoc Investigative Committee, "Exhibit F," 3.
2 Marc Lamont Hill, *Nobody: Casualties of America's War on the Vulnerable*, 184.
3 Eddie S. Glaude Jr. *Democracy in Black*, 10–22, 122–41.
4 Ibid., 172.
5 Michael Eric Dyson, *The Black Presidency*, 66–68.

CHAPTER 1: THE TOWN

1 Stokely Carmichael, "What We Want," review of *The Price of Dissent: Testimonies to Political Repression in America*, by Bud and Ruth Schultz, *New York Review of Books*, September 22, 1966, 216.
2 Jeffrey O. G. Ogbar, *Black Power*, 64.
3 Huey P. Newton, *Huey Newton Speaks*.
4 David Schuyler, *A City Transformed*, 241.
5 Russ Vollmer, "Class of 1962 History," 1.
6 Ibid., 1.
7 Schuyler, *A City Transformed*, 242.
8 David Schuyler, personal interview; David Schuyler, *Urban Renewal and the Changing Face of Lancaster*; Benjamin Bethea, personal interview; University of Virginia, Federal Census Browser (www2.lib.virginia.edu/), 2012.
9 Schuyler, *A City Transformed*, 124.
10 Schuyler, personal interview; General Neighborhood Renewal Plan Application for Adams-Musser Towns Project, 2–3, 8–38, 39–45; Schuyler, *A City Transformed*, 124–27.

11 The present-day Martin Luther King Elementary School replaced the Higbee Elementary School.

12 Schuyler, *A City Transformed*, 153–55; Drayton S. Bryant, *Ongoing Neighborhood Self-Renewal*, 10–21, 61.

13 Schuyler, *A City Transformed*, 157–61.

14 Ibid., 177; Schuyler, *Urban Renewal*.

15 Ronald Ford, personal interview.

CHAPTER 2: THE STRUGGLE

1 "Organize Colored Welfare Society," *Lancaster (PA) New Era*, June 6, 1923; "Many Own Homes and Take Part in Projects," *New Era*, May 3, 1924.

2 "NAACP leader sees summer of Negro discontent, protests," *Intelligencer Journal* (Lancaster, PA), July 2, 1963.

3 Gerald Wilson, telephone interview, September 6, 2007 and October 7, 2007.

4 Elizabeth Ford, personal interview.

5 "Demonstrations again called here by NAACP," *Intelligencer Journal*, July 23, 1963; "NAACP planning for more downtown demonstrations," *Intelligencer Journal*, July 22, 1963.

6 Shirley Lucas Gillis, telephone interview.

7 "NAACP to demonstrate at 2 stores," *Intelligencer Journal*, July 20, 1963.

8 Ford, personal interview.

9 "NAACP plans expansion here for rights push," *Intelligencer Journal*, July 24, 1963.

10 "NAACP sets up meeting with 2 local stores," *Intelligencer Journal*, July 26, 1963; "Demonstrations to end at two stores," *Intelligencer Journal*, July 27, 1963.

11 Leroy Hopkins, personal interview; Shirley Gillis (Lucas), telephone interview.

12 Hopkins, personal interview; Ramilee Washington (Brown), telephone interview.

13 "NAACP plans 2 marches at Rocky Springs," *Intelligencer Journal*, August 3, 1963.

14 "NAACP Plans March Against Pool at Rocky," *Lancaster New Era*, July 30, 1963.

15 Ibid.

16 Hopkins, personal interview.

17 "NAACP Stages Rocky Springs Demonstration," *Lancaster New Era*, August 3, 1963; "Vandals paint Bethel Church," *Intelligencer Journal*, August 5, 1963.

18 "Bethel AME Pastor Honored," *Lancaster New Era*, July 15, 1963; "Bethel AME church honors its new pastor," *Intelligencer Journal*, July 15, 1963.

19 "Lancaster's NAACP Leaders, Kenneth K. Bost, President of Local Chapter," *Lancaster New Era*, August 12, 1963.

20 Hopkins, personal interview; "Rights marchers at pool explain what it's about," *Intelligencer Journal*, August 12, 1963.

21 J. Donald Schaeffer, personal interview; Hopkins, personal interview; Lancaster County Historical Society, "Lancaster at Play," 6–9.

CHAPTER 3: THE DISCONTENT

1 Benjamin Bethea, personal interview.

2 Benjamin F. Bethea Jr. obituary, *LancasterOnline*, August 14, 2013, http://lancasteronline.com/obituaries/benjamin-f-bethea-jr/article_28c12f76-a5d7-5229-ade9-bc576ea48de3.html#.UgtqGC2vTxg.email.

3 Bobby Seale, *Seize the Time*, 70–71.

4 "Thoughts of 2 Youths Accused of Murder," *Intelligencer Journal*, October 25, 1968.

5 John H. Johnson, ed., "Whatever Happened To: Robert F. Williams?" *Ebony* (December 1972), 202.

6 Brown, telephone interview.

7 Bethea, personal interview; David Schuyler, personal interview; David Schuyler, *Urban Renewal and the Changing Face of Lancaster*, 153.

8 Bethea, personal interview.

9 Ibid.

10 Ibid.

11 Ibid.

12 "Thoughts of 2 Youths Accused of Murder."

13 Ibid.

14 "Hire Black Defense Lawyer, CAP Urged," *Intelligencer Journal*, October 25, 1968; "Thoughts of 2 Youths Accused of Murder."

15 Bethea, personal interview.

16 Stan Lathan, *Say Brother*.

CHAPTER 4: THE AFRO-AMERICAN SOCIETY

1 Pauline Pittenger (Leet), personal interview, January 14, 2014; Pre-College Residential Enrichment Program at Franklin and Marshall College, "An Experimental Approach in Education for the Culturally Disadvantaged" (Office of Special Programs, 1964).

2 Franklin and Marshall College, "PREP: The Pre-College Enrichment Program at F&M"; Pittenger, personal interview, February 4, 2014.

3 Franklin and Marshall College, "PREP: The Pre-College Enrichment Program at F&M"; "PREP Aids High Schoolers; Tries to Provide Motivation," *College Reporter* (Lancaster, PA), September 15, 1967; "PREP Pins Financial Hopes on 'Blood, Sweat, and Tears,'" *College Reporter*, April 15, 1969.

4 Pre-College Residential Enrichment Program, "An Experimental Approach in Education."

5 Leon "Buddy" Glover, personal interview.

6 "SWOP Continues Poverty Battle," *College Reporter*, September 26, 1967; Pittenger, personal interview, February 4, 2014.

7 Pittenger, personal interview, February 4, 2014; Barry Chad, "Pauline Leet Defends PREP; Claims 'Too Early' to Judge," *College Reporter*, March 12, 1968.

8 Marianne Clay, "Prepsters of the Past," 18–20.

9 Pittenger, personal interview, February 4, 2014.

10 Glover, personal interview; Clay, "Prepsters of the Past," 18–20.

11 Pittenger, personal interview, February 4, 2014.

12 "Who's Who in Prep," *Prep Star* 1, no. 3 (August 8, 1966): 1; Franklin and Marshall College, Office of Special Programs, *Prepster Yearbook*, 1967, 1.

13 Pittenger, personal interview, January 14, 2014.

14 Lewis H. Myers, telephone interview, January 22, 2014.

15 Glover, personal interview.

16 LeRoy Pernell, telephone interview.

17 Lewis H. Myers, "The Black Student at F&M," 4–5.

18 Myers, telephone interview, February 13, 2014; David M. Stameshkin, *A History of Fraternities and Sororities at Franklin and Marshall College, 1854–1987*, 5–6.

19 Pernell, telephone interview.

20 Benjamin P. Bowser, telephone interview.

21 Myers, "The Black Student at F&M," 6.

22 Franklin and Marshall College, Afro-American Society Folder, 3.

23 Myers, telephone interview, February 13, 2014; Myers, "The Black Student at F&M," 6–7.

24 Pernell, telephone interview.

25 Bowser, telephone interview.

26 Samuel Jordan, "Strategy of Non-Violence Dies at Anti-War March," *College Reporter*, October 27, 1967; Samuel Jordan, "Black Athletes' Olympic Boycott Arouses Dissent," *College Reporter*, December 1, 1967.

27 Angela Davis, *An Autobiography*, 195–223.

28 Myers, telephone interview, January 22, 2014.

29 Bowser, telephone interview.

30 Samuel Jordan and Fania Davis married in 1969. They later divorced in Alameda, California, December 4, 1979 (California Divorce Index, 1966–1984 [database online, the Generations Network Inc., Provo, UT: 2007).

31 James Craighead, personal interview.

32 John J. Johnson, ed., *Jet Magazine* 39, no. 14 (December 31, 1970): 5.

33 Sam Hernandez, "Mohammad Ali Scheduled to Address Afro-American Society This Morning," *College Reporter*, March 5, 1968; Sam Hernandez, "Ali Cites Separation as Hope for Negro," *College Reporter*, March 8, 1968.

34 Bowser, telephone interview.

35 "Negroes Create Group for Political Purposes," *College Reporter*, May 5, 1967; "SWOP Seeking New Volunteers for Coming Year," *College Reporter*, September 23, 1966; "SWOP Prepares Programs for This Summer's Projects," *College Reporter*, February 13, 1968.

36 Craighead, personal interview; Franklin and Marshall College, *Bulletin of Franklin & Marshall College*, 56; George Franklin, telephone interview.

37 Lew Thrash, "Racial Harmony," *College Reporter*, November 5, 1968; Lew Thrash, "A Subterfuge," *College Reporter*, October 8, 1968.

38 "Myers Travels to Urban Schools for Black Student Recruitment," *College Reporter*, February 7, 1969; "Society Plans Black Culture Day," *College Reporter*, October 31, 1969; "Black Studies," *College Reporter*, April 29, 1969; "New Afro-American President Plans More Effective Action," *College Reporter*, April 26, 1968.

39 Pernell, telephone interview; Franklin, telephone interview.

40 Pernell, telephone interview.

41 Myers, telephone interview, January 22, 2014.

42 Glover, personal interview; Myers, telephone interview, January 22, 2014.

43 Tom Gilmore, "Afro-American Society, Prospectus."

44 "Organization Seeks Black Studies," *Campus Reporter* (Lancaster, PA): April 15, 1969.

45 Bowser, telephone interview.

46 Gilmore, "Afro-American Society, Prospectus"; Afro-American Society Academic Committee, "Memorandum."

47 Myers, telephone interview, January 22, 2014.

48 Ben Bowser and Lewis Thrash, "Dear Black Alumni," December 13, 1968; Franklin and Marshall College, Afro-American Society Folder, 2.

49 Afro-American Society, "Black Culture Center"; "Blacks Submit Proposal for Center to Senate," *Campus Reporter*, February 3, 1970; Arthur McClanahan, "Group Proposes Schnader Site for Black Center, Museum," *Campus Reporter*, April 3, 1970.

50 Lewis Thrash, *The Black Collegian*, November 1969.

51 Craighead, personal interview.

52 Franklin and Marshall College, Afro-American Society Folder, 2.

53 *The Black Collegiate*'s name was changed to *The Black Collegian* in 1969 and 1970. Bowser, *The Black Collegiate*, December 2, 1968.

54 "Revolt Shuts Down Howard University," *The Cumberland (MD) News*, March 21, 1968, 1; "Howard U. Protest Ends," *Southern Illinoisan* (Carbondale), March 25, 1928, 14.

55 "Black Power only part of student rebellion," *Southern Illinoisan*, March 25, 1928, 14.

CHAPTER 5: THE CRISIS

1 "Carmichael Calls for Retaliation," *Prescott (AZ) Evening Courier*, April 5, 1968, 1.

2 "Assassination Starts Wave of Negro Violence," *Lancaster (PA) New Era*, April 5, 1968.

3 "12 Cases of Vandalism Burglary Reported Here," *Lancaster New Era*, April 5, 1968.

4 Louis Butcher, personal interview; Benjamin Bethea, personal interview; Leon "Buddy" Glover, personal interview.

5 "Negro Students Express Grief in Somber March," *Lancaster New Era*, April 5, 1968.

6 Gerald Wilson, telephone interview, September 6, 2007, and October 7, 2007.

7 "Negro Students Express Grief in Somber March."

8 Ibid.

9 Benjamin Bowser, telephone interview.

10 Ibid.

11 Andrew Green, "Restraint, Violence Advocated at Vigil for Martin Luther King," *College Reporter* (Lancaster, PA), April 9, 1968; "New Afro-American President Plans More Effective Action," *College Reporter*, April 26, 1968.

12 "Mayor Orders Curfew for City," *Intelligencer Journal* (Lancaster, PA), April 6, 1968; "City Curbs Crowds After Stoning and Looting in S.E. Area," *Lancaster New Era*, April 6, 1968.

13 "City Curbs Crowds After Stoning and Looting in S.E. Area."

14 Ibid.

15 "Violence Results in Police Alert: Firebombs Hit Draft Office," *Intelligencer Journal*, May 11, 1968.

16 Bethea, personal interview.

17 J. Donald Schaeffer, personal interview.

18 Glover, personal interview.

19 "City Curbs Crowds After Stoning."

20 "Local Guard in Limited Call," *Lancaster New Era*, April 9, 1968; Schaeffer, personal interview.

21 Rev. Ernest Ellsworth Christian (June 15, 1909–December 25, 1984) moved to Lancaster in 1928. He died at his home on Christmas Day after battling a long illness.

"Flashback Lancaster: This Week in Lancaster County History," *Lancaster New Era*, December 21, 2009; National Archives and Records Administration, "U.S. World War II Army Enlistment Records, 1938–1946" (database online, Provo, UT). Ancestry.com Operations Inc., 2005. World War II Army Enlistment Records; Records of the National Archives and Records Administration, Record Group 64; National Archives at College Park, MD.

22   Louis Butcher, personal interview.

23   "Dr. King Eulogized at Services Here," *Lancaster New Era*, April 8, 1968.

24   "6 Charged After School Disorders," *Lancaster New Era*, November 1, 1968; Gerald Wilson, telephone interview, October 7, 2007.

CHAPTER 6: THE EXPLOSION

1   "Violence Results in Police Alert: Firebombs Hit Draft Office," *Intelligencer Journal* (Lancaster, PA), May 11, 1968.

2   "Jordan Testifies Was Peacemaker," *Intelligencer Journal*, September 20, 1968, 1, 8.

3   "Two Campus Groups Raising Funds for Jordan's Defense," *College Reporter* (Lancaster, PA), May 14, 1968; Gerald Wilson, telephone interview, October 7, 2007.

4   "Violence Results in Police Alert."

5   Benjamin P. Bowser, telephone interview.

6   Hubert R. Martin and Robert V. Rivers, "Black People's Defense League," May 1968; "Two Campus Groups Raising Funds for Jordan's Defense"; "Jordan Out As Bail Is Reduced," *Intelligencer Journal*, May 14, 1968.

7   "Sam Jordan Wounded, Held for Trying to Kill Officer," *Intelligencer Journal*, November 19, 1969; Keith Spalding, "Statement Regarding Sam Jordan by President Keith Spalding," *Black Liberation Archive*, accessed April 17, 2016, http://blacklib1969.swarthmore.edu/items/show/1179.

8   "Jordan Given Prison Term of 1 to 2 Years," *Lancaster New Era*, April 18, 1969, 1–2; "Jordan Says Role Was Peacemaker," *Intelligencer Journal*, September 20, 1968, 1–8.

9   "Jordan Testifies Was Peacemaker."

10 "Jordan Found Guilty on Gun, Bomb Charges," *Lancaster New Era*, September 23, 1968, 1–2.

11 "Jordan Given Prison Term of 1 to 2 Years"; "Jordan Surrenders; Begins Jail Term," *Lancaster New Era*, December 5, 1970, 1; "Jordan to Be Released," *Lancaster New Era*, February 3, 1972, 1.

12 "Racial Disorder Shuts M'Caskey: 2 Students and a Policeman Are Hurt in Scuffles," *Lancaster New Era*, October 31, 1968. Wilson, telephone interview, September 6, 2007; "6 Charged After School Disorders," *Lancaster New Era*, November 1, 1968.

13 Nancy Val-Kambourglos, personal interview.

14 "Disciplinary Action Slated in Wake of McCaskey Unrest," *Lancaster New Era*, November 1, 1968.

15 Ibid.

16 "Black, White Free Exchange of Ideas Urged," *Lancaster New Era*, November 1, 1968.

17 Benjamin Bethea, personal interview; "McCaskey to Play," *Lancaster New Era*, November 1, 1968.

18 J. Donald Schaeffer, personal interview.

19 "Hearing Set for Three on Riot Charges," *Lancaster New Era*, November 4, 1968; Schaeffer, personal interview.

20 Neither of the Lancaster newspapers made it clear whether the agitator was a student or member of the community, but certain interviewees claim it was Benjamin Bethea.

21 Bethea, personal interview.

22 "8 Policemen Hurt in Stadium Fray," *Lancaster (PA) Sunday News*, November 3, 1968; "Hearings Nov. 12 for 3 Youths," *Intelligencer Journal*, November 5, 1968.

23 "McCaskey to Play"; "Riot Charges Filed against 3 More Youths," *Lancaster New Era*, November 6, 1968; Bethea, personal interview.

24 "Hearing Set for Three on Riot Charges"; Fred Reed, personal interview; "Disciplinary Action Slated in Wake of McCaskey Unrest," *Lancaster New Era*, November 1, 1968; "16 Pupils Suspended for McCaskey Turmoil," *Lancaster New Era*, November 2, 1968.

25 Bethea was exonerated of all but one of the charges.

26 Reed, personal interview.

CHAPTER 7: THE BLACK STUDIES PROPOSAL

1 "Curriculum Committee Requests Elaboration of Black Studies," *College Reporter* (Lancaster, PA), April 25, 1969.

2 LeRoy Pernell, "Black Studies," *College Reporter* (Lancaster, PA), April 29, 1969.

3 Ad Hoc Investigative Committee, "Lewis H. Myers, Full-Credit Course—Black Reality Sent to Faculty at F&M on August 27, 1968," May 21–22, 1969, Buddy Glover Files, Lancaster, PA, 1.

4 Ad Hoc Investigative Committee, "Lewis H. Myers," 2–4.

5 LeRoy Pernell, "Pernell Raps Black Courses," *College Reporter*, February 4, 1969.

6 Pernell, telephone interview.

7 David L. Katz, "Katz Answers Pernell Charges," *College Reporter*, February 7, 1969.

8   Lewis Myers, "Luncheon Interview"; Lewis H. Myers, telephone interview.

9   Ad Hoc Investigative Committee, "Critical Analysis, First Revision," 1.

10   Gerald E. Enscoe, letter to Donald Western, 3.

11   "Curriculum Committee Requests Elaboration of Black Studies," *College Reporter*, April 25, 1969.

12   Benjamin P. Bowser, telephone interview.

13   Ibid.

14   Ad Hoc Investigative Committee, "Critical Analysis, First Revision," 2.

15   "F&M Profs Yield to Black Demands," *Intelligencer Journal*, May 23, 1969.

CHAPTER 8: THE FISHBOWL

1   "Swarthmore Sit-In Ended After Death of Dr. Smith," *Delaware County Daily Times* (Chester, PA), January 17, 1969, 1.

2   "Angela's Sister Fears for Her Life; Husband Faces Jail Sentence," *Jet* (December 31, 1970), 5; "Sam Jordan on Scene at Swarthmore Clash," *Intelligencer Journal* (Lancaster, PA), January 11, 1969; "Police Fail to Find Missing Red in Canada," *Lebanon (PA) Daily News*, August 25, 1970, 14.

3   Donald J. Tyrrell, personal interview.

4   Franklin and Marshall College, "Course Syllabus, the Black Experience in America."

5   Leon Galis, e-mail correspondence.

6   Franklin and Marshall College, "Course Syllabus, the Black Experience in America."

7   Ad Hoc Investigative Committee, Professor Otudeko, "Exhibit C: Black Experience in America Examination Questions."

8   Franklin and Marshall College, "Course Syllabus, the Black Experience in America."

9   Ad Hoc Investigative Committee, "The Report of the Incident at Franklin & Marshall, May 22, 1969," 5.

10   Leon Galis, report to the Ad Hoc Investigative Committee, 3–4.

11   Gerald E. Enscoe, letter to Donald Western, 6.

12   Ibid., 7.

13   Galis, e-mail correspondence.

14   Ibid.

15   Ibid.

16   Louis Butcher, personal interview.

17   Paul Feldsher, "Enscoe Presents Defense of Radical at First Forum," *College Reporter*, November 8, 1966; Gerald L. Bresslour, "Enscoe Discusses Issues; Seeks End to Vietnam War," *College Reporter*, September 29, 1967; Russ Vollmer, "Class of 1962 History," 1; "Petition to Stress Swift Viet Pullout,"

College Reporter, October 24, 1969; "Students Supporting RFK Form Committee," *College Reporter*, October 21, 1966.

18 Brett Harwood, letter to Donald Western.

19 Benjamin P. Bowser, telephone interview.

20 Ad Hoc Investigative Committee, "Critical Analysis, First Revision," 4. In 1967, the faculty at F&M passed a motion that allowed students to take up to four courses under a pass/no pass system, and also voted to change the rank-in-class system from a number to "high to low rank-in-class."

21 Enscoe, letter to Donald Western, 8.

22 Ibid.

23 Galis, report to the Ad Hoc Investigative Committee, 8–9.

24 Ibid., 9.

25 "Campus Unrest Shifts to Cornell," *Montana Record* (Helena, MT), April 20, 1969, 1; "Sit-In at Cornell University Ended by Armed Black Students," *Times Recorder* (Zanesville, OH), April 21, 1969, 1.

26 "Guns Across a Yawning Racial Gulf," *Bennington (VT) Banner*, April 22, 1969, 4.

27 "Big Tuition-Free College, CCNY, Is Closed by Militant Students," *Kane (PA) Republican*, April 23, 1969, 1.

28 Ad Hoc Investigative Committee, "Critical Analysis, First Revision," 4.

29 Myers, telephone interview, January 22, 2014.

30 Enscoe, 8.

31 Ad Hoc Investigative Committee, "Critical Analysis, First Revision," 6.

32 Lewis Myers, "Luncheon Interview," 25.

33 Bowser, telephone interview.

34 The Black Students of Interdepartmental-4 and the Black Students at Franklin and Marshall, "Position Paper: Black Students of Interdepartmental-Four," 1.

35 Ad Hoc Investigative Committee, "Exhibit E."; "F&M Profs Yield to Black Demands," *Intelligencer Journal*, May 23, 1969; "F&M Yields to Blacks' Refusal to Take Exam," *Lancaster New Era*, May 23, 1969.

36 Enscoe, 10.

37 Donald Western et al., "Final Report of the Ad Hoc Investigative Committee," 1–2.

38 Galis, report to the Ad Hoc Investigative Committee, 2.

39 Enscoe, 10.

40 Galis, e-mail correspondence.

41 Ad Hoc Investigative Committee, "The Report of the Incident at Franklin & Marshall, May 22, 1969," 6–9; Enscoe, 10; George Franklin, telephone interview.

42 Galis, report to the Ad Hoc Investigative Committee, 1.

43 Ad Hoc Investigative Committee, "Critical Analysis, First Revision," 4.

CHAPTER 9: THE UPRISING

1   Dick Preston, letter to Donald Western; Ad Hoc Investigative Committee, Frederic F. Klein, meeting minutes, May 22, 1969, Buddy Glover Files, Lancaster, PA, 2.

2   Henry Farrington, letter to Donald Western.

3   Donald Western et al., "Final Report of the Ad Hoc Investigative Committee"; "F&M Yields to Blacks' Refusal to Take Exam," *Lancaster (PA) New Era*, May 23, 1969; Ad Hoc Investigative Committee, "The Report of the Incident at Franklin & Marshall, May 22, 1969," 8.

4   Harold Dunbar, telephone interview.

5   Donald J. Tyrrell, personal interview.

6   Franklin and Marshall College, Bruce G. Holran, Director of Public Relations, "Press Release," December 31, 1969, 3.

7   F. J. Murray, letter to Donald Western.

8   Ibid.

9   Ibid.

10   Ad Hoc Investigative Committee, "Critical Analysis, First Revision," 5.

11   Leon Galis, e-mail correspondence.

12   Dick Preston, letter to Donald Western.

13   Ibid.

14   Alan Eisen, letter to Donald Western; James Craighead, personal interview.

15   Mitchell Brecher, letter to the Ad Hoc Investigative Committee.

16   Richard Rementer, letter to Donald Western.

17   Brett Harwood, letter to Donald Western.

18   Murray, letter to Donald Western.

19   "F&M Yields to Blacks' Refusal to Take Exam," *Lancaster New Era*, May 23, 1969; "F&M Profs Yield to Black Demands," *Intelligencer Journal*, May 23, 1969.

20   Lewis Myers, "Luncheon Interview," 7.

21   Ibid., 7–8.

22   LeRoy Pernell, telephone interview.

23   Ad Hoc Investigative Committee, "Critical Analysis, First Revision," 6.

24   James H. Gordon, letter to the Ad Hoc Investigative Committee regarding "Recollections of events of May 22, 1969."

25   Dick Preston, letter to Donald Western; Galis, e-mail correspondence.

26   Leon Galis, report to the Ad Hoc Investigative Committee, 6.

27   Louis Athey et al., "To the Community," 2.

28   Ad Hoc Investigative Committee, "Exhibit F."

29   Ibid.

30   Gordon, letter to the Ad Hoc Investigative Committee.

31   Preston, letter to Donald Western.

32   Dunbar, telephone interview; "Student Takeover Ends at Swarthmore," *Black Liberation 1969 Archive*, accessed October 9, 2015, http://blacklib1969. swarthmore.edu/items/show/644.

33   Galis, report to the Ad Hoc Investigative Committee, 5; Klein, meeting minutes, 4.

34   Tyrrell, personal interview.

35   Myers, "Luncheon Interview," 2.

36   Pernell, telephone interview.

37   Preston, letter to Donald Western.

38   Tyrrell, personal interview.

39   Galis, report to the Ad Hoc Investigative Committee, 6.

CHAPTER 10: THE INVESTIGATION

1   Leon Galis, report to the Ad Hoc Investigative Committee, 3.

2   Ibid., 5.

3   Ibid., 6.

4   "F&M Profs Yield to Black Demands," *Intelligencer Journal* (Lancaster, PA), May 23, 1969; Frederic S. Klein, meeting minutes, 5.

5   "Senate at F&M Balks at Bowing," *Intelligencer Journal*, May 29, 1969; Galis, report to the Ad Hoc Investigative Committee, 7.

6   Leon Galis, e-mail correspondence.

7   "F&M Takes Stand on Campus," *Intelligencer Journal*, May 27, 1969; "F&M Won't Tolerate Violent Disruptions," *Lancaster (PA) New Era*, May 26, 1969.

8   "Graduate Concerned with Demand for 'A.' Letter to the Editor, Mildly Upset," *Lancaster New Era*, May 27, 1969.

9   Concerned Alumnus, "F&M Capitulation Seen Inept Action," *Lancaster New Era*, May 28, 1969.

10   Jack Flom, letter to the College Senate, 1–2; Alan Eisen et al. "To College Senate."

11   "Full F&M Faculty Reverses 7 Profs On 'No Grading,'" *Lancaster New Era*, May 29, 1969.

12   Secretary of the College Senate, "To the Faculty," May 27, 1969, Buddy Glover Files, Lancaster, PA, 2.

13   Ad Hoc Investigative Committee, "The Report of the Incident at Franklin & Marshall, May 22, 1969," 10–11.

14   "F&M Throws Out Grading Decision," *Intelligencer Journal*, May 29, 1969.

15   Ad Hoc Investigative Committee, "The following is a resolution passed by unanimous vote," July 1, 1969, Buddy Glover Files, Lancaster, PA.

16   Lew Myers is quoted in the report by Donald Western et al., "Final Report of the Ad Hoc Investigative Committee," November 7, 1969, Office of Public

Relations, Franklin and Marshall College, Lancaster, PA; Lewis H. Myers, telephone interview, January 22, 2014.

17 Donald Western et al., "Final Report of the Ad Hoc Investigative Committee."

18 Ad Hoc Investigative Committee, "Critical Analysis," November 27, 1969; flyer distributed to F&M students announcing the Black Experience in America course, fall 1968.

19 Franklin and Marshall College, *Oriflamme* (Lancaster, PA, 1969), 21–23.

20 Africana Studies Program Committee, "Proposal for the Establishment of a Major in Africana Studies," Franklin and Marshall College, Lancaster, PA, January 1999, 2–22; Michael L. Penn, "Proposal of the Africana Studies Program Committee Transition to a Major in Africana Studies."

INDEX

Made in the USA
Middletown, DE
09 January 2019